50

FIFTY YEARS OF
ADVENTURE

Rudolf Abraham
Dan Bailey
Grant Bourne
Ian Boydon
Hamish M Brown
Sandy Brown
Justi Carey
Alan Castle
Roy Clark

Rachel Crolla
Chiz Dakin
Paddy Dillon
Mike Dunn
Aileen Evans
Brian Evans
Bob Gibbons
Allan Hartley
Leigh Hatts

Alan Hinkes
Rob Houghton
Tony Howard
Guy Hunter-Watts
Will Janecek
Brian Johnson
Kingsley Jones
Bart Jordans
Dennis Kelsall

Radek Kucharski
Terry Marsh
Bill O'Connor
Mike Pescod
Gillian Price
Siân Pritchard-Jones
Kev Reynolds
Mark Richards
James Rushforth

Jim Ryan
Phoebe Smith
Alex Stewart
Ronald Turnbull
Mike Wells
Jeff Williams
Joe Williams
Jonathan Williams
Madeline Williams
Loraine Wilson

First edition 2019
ISBN: 978 1 78631 030 9
Contributing editor: Kev Reynolds

Cicerone
Juniper House, Murley Moss,
Oxenholme Road, Kendal,
Cumbria LA9 7RL
www.cicerone.co.uk

A catalogue record for this book is available
from the British Library.

Printed in China on behalf of Latitude Press Ltd

Mapping by Lovell Johns www.lovelljohns.com
UK relief map: © EuroGeographics. Original
product is freely available at eurogeoarchive.
srgry.uk. Terms of the licence available
at http://eurogeoarchive.srgry.uk/form/
topographic-data-eurogeographics

Cover photo:
Hikers return to Rifugio Locatelli as the Milky Way
hangs above the Tre Cime (James Rushforth)

Endpaper photo credit: Jonathan Williams

Our thanks to Duncan Unsworth for supplying
the photos of Walt and Dorothy Unsworth, and
Brian and Aileen Evans for the photos of their
younger selves.

See page 156 for photo credits and captions not
mentioned in the text.

Contents

Out there: Adventures worldwide

Mishaps and misadventures

An adventurous bunch: Contributing authors

The Cicerone team

Photo credits and captions

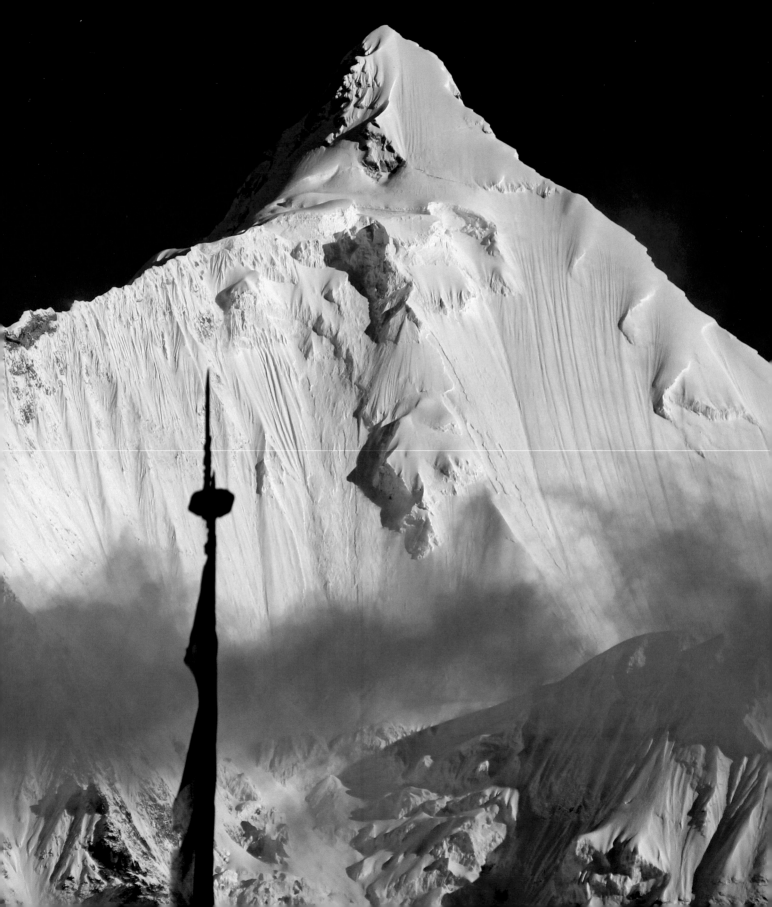

An appreciation

For fifty years, Cicerone have sought to help adventurers have a great and safe experience, be it walking, trekking, climbing, mountaineering, cycling, running or something even more intrepid. This book is an insight into those years, and the adventures along the way. We hope you enjoy reading it as much as we have enjoyed making it.

Our thanks and a big shout-out to our contributing authors – without you it would not have been possible to make this book. You have brought together an interesting – eclectic even – group of outdoor adventures and experiences, from the challenging to the contemplative, from survival experiences to journeys of self-discovery, from the Thames valley to the summit of K2. As ever, you have done a great job.

This is a good place for us to thank all Cicerone authors for their amazing efforts over many years. Creating a great guide is undoubtedly a challenge – it requires knowledge and love of an area, a talent for choosing routes, writing, photographic, cartographic and increasingly digital skills, the ability to bring it all together, for the author's personality to shine through, to be authoritative yet friendly, to be encouraging but careful. The author is the parent of a guide; as the publisher we stand as guardians of the project and to be successful the two must work together in harmony.

Authors are the foundation of any successful publisher, but many others play their part – the office team of editors, designers, sales and marketing, finance and systems, our copyeditors, freelance designers, partners in mapping, digital work, printing, distribution, and sales. It's a team effort and it is a great team. There hasn't been space to mention everyone who has contributed, who wished to write articles, and who has made a great contribution to Cicerone over the years. For those left out, we can only apologise and promise to do better in another fifty years!

We would like to finish with a few personal words. Verity Russo and Caroline Draper have managed to fit this project in around their already busy editorial and design work. Pat Dunn edited with her usual skill. Brian and Aileen Evans as co-founders of Cicerone have been a fount of knowledge on the early days following the deaths of Walt and Dorothy Unsworth in the last 18 months.

And finally, our thanks to Kev Reynolds for helping bring it all together, for taking on the role of contacting authors, reviewing contributions and giving the project a shape. But even more, Kev, our thanks for your company on treks, and your wisdom and friendship over many years.

Jonathan and Lesley Williams

◄ Jitchu Drake (c.6800m), climbed in 1988 by its south face before a ban was imposed on all mountaineering in Bhutan (photo: Bart Jordans)

Prologue

We are sitting outside the Cabane du Mont-Fort high above Verbier, looking out at the sunset over the Combin range with Mont Blanc behind. Dinner is coming soon and the trekkers' thoughts have moved on from today's grinding 1650m climb to tomorrow's route over the wild and remote Grand Désert. The question goes out: 'What does Kev say?' and half a dozen copies of the little blue guidebook appear and are studied. Of course, most of the trekkers have read the book several times, but this is the decision point – whether to take the high path over the Col de la Chaux with the chance of late snow, or the slightly lower Sentier des Chamois with spectacular views of the Combin and the long drop to Val de Bagnes. Plans are made, dinner is served, beers are exchanged for wine, and conversation flows in several languages.

The scene is played out wherever we go: in the Dolomites, the AV2 trekkers at Rifugio Pisciadù are asking 'What does Gillian say?'; the GR20 trekkers at Ascu Stagnu in Corsica are asking 'What does Paddy say?'; the Munroists at the Killin B&B are studying Steve's book or Ronald's, while the West Highland Way walkers in Rowardennan ask what Terry says. Much the same scene happens from the Alps to the Canaries, from Cornwall to the north of Scotland, from Patagonia to the Rockies. Grades are dissected, times and distances computed and checked, the ups and downs investigated, the maps explored for critical turns, the photographs assessed for dodgy terrain. Every word, every comma, matters.

This is what it is all about, why the team works so hard on the guides. The guide truly comes alive where, to borrow from William Blake, 'men [and women] and mountains meet'. We reflect on the responsibility of helping so many adventurers achieve their hills, treks and trips, and we feel the pleasure of helping them do so. In the feedback we receive from walkers and trekkers, we see how every aspect of our craft must play its part, how the exactitude and quality of our authors' work and of our own work must come together perfectly; we see the importance of the highest editorial standards and great design, the best maps and photographs, the constant effort to stay as up to date as possible.

Then we look deeper and see more. We see the importance of finding inspiring new places, ranges and routes; the importance of the author's love and passion and desire to communicate it, which is the foundation of all our work; the importance of how we market and present our guides; the importance of our reputation – our brand, if you like. We look deeper and see the importance of working with great people, of training the team and of their learning; the importance of how we look after customers and how we answer the phone, how we handle a sales visit, how we write a blog, conduct an interview, build a website.

We see the relationships with our partners, our distributors, printers, copy-editors, sales teams. We see the choice of paper, the perfection of the printing, we see the order turnaround times, the delivery accuracy, the quality of the packaging. Deeper still, we see the importance of technology, of managing cash, of good planning, of our daily processes and interactions, of running the business.

And especially we see how the integrity and passion of the team and of our authors, the ideas and relationships, combine with the day-to-day business and hard work to help walkers have days to remember with pleasure. And we reflect on how fortunate we have been to work with such great people for all these years.

'What does Kev say?' In those few words spoken high in the Swiss Alps, the whole of Cicerone is laid bare to us and we see how everything works together – all the moving parts we've strived to perfect and the people we've worked with for a good part of a generation.

Are we proud? Maybe just a little. Are we nervous about our responsibilities? Absolutely. Do we want to keep on doing it better? Definitely.

Jonathan and Lesley Williams

⌃ Chilled feet were guaranteed when crossing a stream
of snowmelt above Berghaus Vereina

⌃ Restoring life to weary legs after the steep descent to Alp Sardasca
(both photos above in the Silvretta by Kev Reynolds)

❯ On a very rugged link route from Grotelle to the Brèche de
Capitellu on Corsica's GR20 (photo: Paddy Dillon)

The Cicerone story
FROM THEN TO NOW

It was the combined talents of two climbers, a Yorkshireman and a Lancastrian, that laid the foundations of Cicerone Press.

A founder member of the Lancashire Mountaineering Club, Walt Unsworth was born in 1928 and began fell walking in the Lake District during World War II, before turning to rock climbing with a weekend base at Wall End Barn in Langdale. An early visit to Norway, an introduction to gorge exploration in the Libyan desert during his national service, and a trip to the Maritime Alps – all this gave him wider vision and a taste for adventure, which led to a further eight Alpine seasons during which he made ascents of classic peaks such as the Matterhorn, Zinalrothorn and the Grand Charmoz.

On the opposite side of the Pennines from Manchester-based Unsworth, Brian Evans became interested in rock climbing while at school in the early 1950s. This interest turned into an obsession, leading to a three-month trip to the Alps in 1962, when he climbed the Cima Grande in the Dolomites, Piz Badile in the Bregaglia and various big routes above Chamonix, including the west face of the Dru. In other Alpine seasons he traversed Monte Rosa, Castor and Pollux, climbed the Obergabelhorn and Zinalrothorn, – and had a long day on the Matterhorn with an ascent of the Hörnli Ridge followed by descent of the Italian flank and a return to Switzerland under the east face.

Meanwhile, Walt married Dorothy Winstanley, a fellow teacher, in 1952. With aspirations as a writer, he managed to balance his teaching career with marriage, raising a family and introducing his pupils to outdoor activities, somehow finding time to write *The Young Mountaineer* in 1959 and *A Climber's Guide to Pontesford Rocks* in 1962. But it was *The English Outcrops*, published by Victor Gollancz in 1964, that brought him to wider attention. Illustrated with photographs and sketch maps, *Outcrops* directed climbers to an eclectic assortment of crags and quarries and was later hailed as 'one of the seminal books of post-war climbing'.

Back across the Pennines, after spending four years at Leeds College of Art and two years at Catterick on national service, Brian found work as an artist and married Aileen Wilby-Newton, a teacher and fellow member of the Yorkshire Mountaineering Club. Thus began a partnership that continues to thrive, with Brian and Aileen still participating in mountain-based adventures some 60 years on. Having returned from his epic 1962 season in the Alps, Brian began a freelance career

Clockwise from top left:
Walt Unsworth, Dolomites, 1976; Dorothy and the children climbing on the glacier, Zermatt, 1964; Brian Evans on Gimmer Crag, Langdale, *c.*1962 (photo: Tony Greenbank); Brian and Aileen Evans, Upper Wortley, Leeds, *c.*1957

15

writing and illustrating articles for various magazines. This led to a long association with *Climber & Rambler*, supported by the editor, Ron Butchart, who month by month would send him articles to illustrate with his lively pen-and-ink drawings. A number of these were written by Walt Unsworth.

When the editor's desk became vacant mid-issue, Walt was asked by the publisher to fill in until a replacement could be found. Despite living near Manchester and the magazine being published in Scotland, he resigned from teaching and made the job his own. Under his astute guidance, the magazine gained a fresh identity, and he increased its circulation while at the same time writing a whole string of books with a mountaineering theme.

In the late 1960s, Walt and Dorothy invited Brian and Aileen to their home. 'How would you like to be a millionaire?' asked Walt with a grin and tongue firmly in cheek. And with that he proposed that the four of them set up a company to publish pocket-sized guidebooks for walkers and climbers under the name of Cicerone, meaning 'a guide'.

By this time, Brian and Aileen had moved to the outskirts of Preston, where Brian bought a small printing press, and it was on this that the early Cicerone guides were produced – the very first being a small, inexpensive climbing guide written by Walt's close friend, teaching colleague and climbing instructor, Arthur Hassall. Financed by both couples, who provided £60 each to cover production costs, *The Northern Lake District* was published in 1969. It consisted of just 40 pages and included hand-drawn illustrations by Brian who, two years later, wrote and illustrated a companion climbing guide, *The Southern Lake District*.

From the very outset, Walt was ambitious and hard-working, supported in his endeavours by his wife. Through his magazine editorship, he had contacts everywhere in the climbing world, enabling him to commission several highly respected names to produce guidebooks for him. Ian Clough was among the earliest to respond, writing what was to become, in 1969, Cicerone's second title: *Winter Climbs: Ben Nevis and Glencoe*. Clough was at the forefront of British mountaineering, with significant first ascents – Central Pillar of Frêney, Eiger (first British ascent of the north face) and Central Tower of Paine in Patagonia – and was a founder of the Glencoe School of Mountaineering. He was tragically killed in an ice avalanche on Annapurna in 1970.

Winter Climbs was an instant success with climbers in search of challenging routes in the Highlands. The format of the guide was the same as Arthur Hassall's Lakeland book, crammed with 50 wire-stitched pages of accessible information in a blue-and-white cover. And it was cheap. Reprint followed reprint – some of its success, it was claimed, being due to the colour of the cover making it difficult to find when dropped in the snow, for climbers would then have to buy

another copy! Following Clough's death, *Winter Climbs* was revised and expanded by Hamish MacInnes in 1971, with another edition appearing in 1978. It has been further developed by some of Scotland's leading climbing educators, Alan Kimber and then Mike Pescod.

Unsworth's vision for Cicerone Press was never limited to British mountains, and one of his earliest approaches was to a climber who had come to the fore by making the first ascent of the formidable Troll Wall in Romsdal, Norway, said to be the highest rock face in Europe. Born in 1940, Tony Howard was active among the limestone crags of Derbyshire and had written the British Mountaineering Council's guide to Chew Valley in 1965, the same year he scaled the Troll Wall. Walt invited him over to his house in Worsley on the edge of Manchester and offered him a contract to write *Walks and Climbs in Romsdal, Norway*. Published in 1970 with 174 pages, it became known in Norway as *den lille blå boken* (the little blue book), inspiring a number of young Norwegians to take up climbing for themselves. (Howard became a founder of Troll climbing equipment, and later developed Wadi Rum in Jordan as a major climbing and trekking destination, which he and Di Taylor describe in *Jordan: Walks, Treks, Caves, Climbs and Canyons* and *Treks and Climbs in Wadi Rum*.)

At first, the Cicerone list grew at a rate of just one or two new titles a year. Highly respected mountaineer and educationist Hamish M Brown's *The Island of Rhum* appeared in 1972, and *Modern Snow and Ice Techniques* by Bill March followed in 1973, along with *Modern Rope Techniques in Mountaineering*. March was perhaps the leading climbing educator of his time, director of the National Mountaineering Centre at Plas y Brenin and leader of the first successful Canadian Everest expedition. Sadly, he died of an aneurysm in 1990 when on a trip with some of his students.

Cicerone's appearance on the outdoor scene had been well timed. The first ascent of Everest in 1953 and the launch of the Duke of Edinburgh's Award scheme in 1956 had stimulated a fresh enthusiasm for outdoor activities that was further encouraged by the Boy Scouts Association. While climbing had been a semi-exclusive activity before the war, by the mid 1960s the mountains of Snowdonia, the Lake District and Scotland thronged with groups and individuals clad in Ventile (cotton) anoraks in search of adventure. Backpacking and long-distance walking came into vogue. The Pennine Way was established, after a lengthy battle, in 1965, and Alfred Wainwright wrote his *Coast to Coast* guidebook in 1973. Those who could afford it took a fortnight's holiday in the Alps, to walk, trek or climb, and Walt and Brian quickly realised that Cicerone should provide guidance. Their guides were intended, after all, to be 'for walkers and climbers, written and produced by walkers and climbers', wherever they might wish to go.

'A company...under the name of Cicerone, meaning "a guide"'

Top row from left:
Dorothy Unsworth, Spelunca;
Aileen Evans (photo: Brian Evans);
Brian Evans (photo: Ian Howell)

Centre: Brian getting to grips
with an early Cicerone guide

Bottom row from left:
Walt Unsworth, national service;
Dorothy Unsworth; Dorothy and
the children, camping 1964

Top row from left:
Tony Howard and Di Taylor; Kev
Reynolds squatting among the
Pyrenees, 1983; Paddy Dillon

Centre: Walt Unsworth

Bottom row from left: Terry Marsh;
Ronald Turnbull; Mark Richards

One day in the mid 1970s, an article arrived in the *Climber & Rambler* in-tray from a recently retired BBC employee describing a trek around Mont Blanc, illustrated with some fine black-and-white photographs. After the article appeared in the magazine, Walt contacted the author asking him to produce a guide to what was already considered to be the finest multi-day trek in the Alps. Sussex-based Andrew Harper accepted the invitation and duly wrote and illustrated a slim, 100-page walking guide, the *Tour of Mont Blanc* (1977), which went through several editions before the author died in 2001. The title was then passed to one of Cicerone's then most prolific authors, Kev Reynolds.

Reynolds was a Pyrenean specialist and a youth hostel warden in Kent, writing magazine articles at night when everyone had gone to bed. Several of his pieces had appeared in *Climber & Rambler* so Walt called him one day with an invitation to write a guide to Europe's second major range west of the Caucasus. Having never used a guidebook before, Reynolds first had to research the kind of information required, before gathering 100 routes for *Walks and Climbs in the Pyrenees*, which appeared in 1978.

As the Cicerone list began to grow, publisher and authors alike became increasingly aware that each successive guidebook marked the beginning of a long-term 'duty of care': it was not simply a matter of producing the books and then forgetting about them. Unlike works of fiction or volumes of history that require no regular updating, a guide to walks, treks or climbs, for example, is of use only as long as the information it provides is accurate and up to date. When route changes occur – either by natural causes such as damage or destruction by rockfall, avalanche or flood, or by man-made diversions or constructions – it falls to the guidebook author to reflect such changes in an updated reprint or a completely new edition. It is this continuity of 'ownership' of a title that makes the work of guidebook author and publisher different from most other forms of publishing.

The guidebook author is like a parent who is responsible for the birth, delivery and continuing care of his or her child – in this case, the guidebook. Both author and publisher nurture it from conception, through infancy and adolescence. Reynolds' *Walks and Climbs in the Pyrenees* is no exception. Forty years on, it is still in print, having grown through many editions and updates from a modest 128 pages, with a small selection of black-and-white photos and line drawings by Brian Evans, to a bulky 412-page tome with colour illustrations throughout.

In 1982, four years after the very first edition of *Walks and Climbs* came out (and when Reynolds was still innocent of his long-term duty of care for its lifetime), Cicerone published another book by the same author: *Mountains of the Pyrenees* was a slim hardback history of

climbing in those mountains. When Reynolds set out to try his hand as a freelance writer in 1986, it was the Unsworth–Evans partnership that supported his efforts with a series of contracts to produce guidebooks for Cicerone, ranging from day walks in southern England to major treks in the Himalaya by way of numerous walks and treks in the European Alps. Although never a staff member, Kev Reynolds was probably the first writer to earn the bulk of his living by producing Cicerone guides.

Unsworth had relinquished his role as editor of *Climber & Rambler* in the late 1970s and moved to Milnthorpe on the edge of the Lake District to concentrate on his own writing career alongside running Cicerone Press. At first, the Cicerone office was briefly housed in the basement of Walt and Dorothy's new home, but it soon moved all of 100 metres to Police Square, where the conversion of two 100-year-old cottages provided more spacious accommodation for the growing business. Dorothy had retired from teaching and was now running the day-to-day operations, while Walt commissioned and edited new books that were designed and printed in Preston by Brian and Aileen Evans under the banner of Carnmor Print and Design. In Milnthorpe, additional members of staff were taken on to handle orders and look after customers.

'Their guides were... "for walkers and climbers, written and produced by walkers and climbers"'

Ever energetic, Walt helped found the Outdoor Writers Guild (now the Outdoor Writers and Photographers Guild) in 1979, so establishing a long relationship between Cicerone and leading UK-based outdoor writers. Supporting the Guild throughout its existence, whether by introducing new authors to the Guild or by working with existing Guild members, Cicerone has contributed to excellence in outdoor writing over many years. Many of its authors – Terry Marsh, Mark Richards, Ronald Turnbull, Paddy Dillon, to name but a few – have been Guild members.

Over the next 20 years, Cicerone attracted a range of authors and would-be authors who approached Walt with ideas for guides to their own favourite location and activity. An expanding catalogue of titles, and a wish list of areas to include, was matched by a pile of unsolicited manuscripts and book proposals that began to grow on the editor's desk, so that by the time Walt, Dorothy, Brian and Aileen began to plan their retirement, they could look with satisfaction on bookshelves groaning with more than 280 guidebooks, promising days of adventure in the great outdoors.

In 1999, 30 years after its birth on the outskirts of Manchester, a healthy Cicerone Press was sold to Jonathan and Lesley Williams, a 40-ish couple with professional backgrounds, with no publishing experience but a shared passion for outdoor activity, an abundance of ideas and a determination to build on the success achieved by Walt and Dorothy Unsworth and Brian and Aileen Evans.

Coming into the business with no prior experience of book production was, perhaps, to the benefit of the new owners, who claim that what could have been a disadvantage was turned to advantage. As Jonathan explained: 'We had the "luxury" of learning everything from scratch and were able to build from first principles, to make it up as we went along!' In other words, they got to learn by their mistakes.

Raised in Yorkshire, Jonathan was a chartered accountant, while Lesley was from Wallingford in Oxfordshire (although in good Cicerone tradition she has a Lancastrian heritage too), with a background in retailing and marketing. They met while sailing across the Bay of Biscay with the Island Cruising Club and married three years later in 1983.

As a geography student at Southampton University, Lesley had spent a summer studying the glaciers above Arolla, and the year after they married, she and Jonathan returned to Switzerland for a walking holiday based in the tiny Alpine village with which she had become familiar. After that, the Alps were to become a regular holiday destination (on top of snatched weekends in the Lakes and summer weeks in Scotland). It was through a chance meeting on a Chamonix campsite several years later that the idea of turning the focus of their careers towards outdoor adventure began to germinate.

Sharing that campsite was Walt and Dorothy Unsworth's son Duncan, who was there with his wife and children – one of whom had been to nursery school with Jonathan and Lesley's daughter. Mention of Cicerone guidebooks came into conversation – the Williamses already had several on their shelves at home – and the connection with Duncan's parents became apparent. Jonathan and Lesley were evaluating their next career and life steps, and it was clear that Cicerone fitted with these plans. The pieces of a jigsaw puzzle began to form a picture of possibilities…

Less than a year later, the following brief press release was issued:

> From the end of May [1999], Cicerone Press, the well-known guidebook firm, comes under new ownership. Founded 30 years ago by Walt Unsworth and Brian Evans, the firm, specialising in the great outdoors, now has more than 250 titles spanning the whole of Britain and many areas of the world. The new company will be Cicerone Press Ltd, whose MD is Jonathan Williams. It will operate from the same address in Cumbria.

Letters advising authors of the change of ownership were considerably less formal than that official announcement, and included a paragraph saying: 'premises remain the same, and business will be conducted as before. Contracts remain in force and royalties will be paid as previously' – to which many Cicerone authors breathed a sigh of relief and said 'Amen!'

The new owners inherited a small team: Hilary Bentley, Gina Varcoe and a little part-time editorial and secretarial support. Hilary and Gina were stalwarts of those early years, although the cultural change from 'Mrs Unsworth' to Jonathan encouraging them to 'press buttons on the keyboard to find out what the computer can do' was a broad chasm for them to cross. Gina retired after a couple of years, while Hilary retired in 2006 after 21 years with Cicerone. It was an interesting time, and the team faced a series of learning curves, including having to master complex computer programs at the rate of about one a month. But the main task was to build the team, capabilities and resources.

In late 2000, Hilary was trekking in Nepal, Gina had fallen ill, and Lesley was definitely feeling the strain when Jonathan came in from a sales trip one wet day and found Clare Crooke (now the longest-serving member of the team) packing books. Clare had spotted Lesley's cry for help in the office window and, although it had little to do with her background in advertising and design, she knocked on the door and was put to work there and then. She soon found herself parcelling and distributing guidebooks and answering the telephone. Clare's real passion was for design, so she enrolled in an evening class to study computer software used for designing books, and before long was able to exchange parcel tape for a computer in the design team where she remains to this day – nearly 20 years on!

Under the new owners, Cicerone has been fortunate in attracting three remarkable editorial managers, the first of whom was Hazel Clarke, succeeded by Lois Sparling and then Andrea Grimshaw. Before relocating to the Lake District, Hazel had worked at Oxford University Press on both the *Oxford English Dictionary* and the renowned *Oxford Dictionary of National Biography*. She had also written and produced works on environmental issues, so by the time she arrived in Milnthorpe she was well versed in editorial standards and had a sound publishing background. Given a room to herself, Hazel would take care of the editing, create layouts, choose photographs and try to make sense of the maps before sending everything to the printers. Meanwhile, Jonathan was getting to grips with each stage of guidebook production and Lesley was busy with sales and marketing.

Hazel remembers the anxious wait for books to come back from the printers: 'Is it all we've dreamed of?'

'Well, it looks like a book!'

Jonathan recalls long hours studying every aspect of preparing a guidebook, from idea through to updated second and third editions, and devising a doctrine and processes that would stand the test of time and consistently create outstanding guides. Lesley remembers the challenge of marketing on less than a shoestring, managing several hundred customers, humping books around and trying to get the

'…the team faced a series of learning curves'

initially unpredictable end of the production process to somehow link up with the start of her sales and marketing efforts.

The 'new' Cicerone had inherited a few half-finished books, some with very troublesome maps. One in particular was a guide to walks in an East European country, with old Russian army maps to work from. After trying to find alternatives for several years, the team eventually had to accept that there were no others in existence, so the only option was to adapt the Russian maps and hope there would be no arrests for printing state secrets!

Harold Macmillan spoke about 'events' derailing the best-laid plans. And while the steady hard work of production and marketing continued, it was the crises that forged the team and the necessary decision-making into a new and tougher shape, and it is the crises that stick firmly in the memory.

Only two weeks after Jonathan and Lesley took over, news came of the death of Cicerone author Constance Roos. Born in San Francisco, Constance was a widely travelled hiker and climber, author of *Walking in Norway*, and Assistant Clinical Professor of Psychiatry at the University of California. Struck by lightning while researching a guide to the GR20 in Corsica, her death cast a very long shadow.

Less than two years later, in February 2001, just as the new team was beginning to grow in confidence, the British countryside was virtually closed down by foot-and-mouth disease. With tens of thousands of footpaths and bridleways placed off-limits, sales of guidebooks plummeted. Suddenly, everything related to outdoor activity in Britain was put on hold, as were Cicerone's plans. It was a grim period, not only for farmers, the countryside and tourist infrastructure but also for publishers of walking guides. For Jonathan and Lesley, it provided time to take stock and plan ahead, so that Cicerone was able to emerge from the crisis with vision, energy and solid plans for the future.

After a year's closure, the countryside gradually reopened and walkers flooded in like bees to flowers. Timed to coincide, the first Outdoors Show was held at the National Exhibition Centre in Birmingham. It was an extraordinary event to which trail-hungry walkers flocked in their thousands, giving a real boost to all involved in the great outdoors. Cicerone had booked a small stand at the show and, within moments of the doors opening, it was swamped by an eager guidebook-buying public – so much so that a panic phone call was made by Lesley to the Milnthorpe office: 'Bring books!' was the instruction.

'Which ones?'

'Anything, just bring books, as many as you can. We've almost sold out!'

Confidence returned, and the process of building the Cicerone team continued. As the team grew, individual jobs became more specialised. New members of staff took over the layout, map work and production, in order that Hazel could concentrate on copy-editing the text; later, the editing went out to freelancers and Hazel became the editorial manager, her role being to manage the whole editorial process. She says: 'It was always a close team – physically close (nearly all in one room) – and we worked very closely together – with all the joys and frustrations that can bring! However, it was true to say that everyone cared very much about the books and wanted each one to be as good as it possibly could be.'

Space doesn't allow everyone's story to be told, but as an author I can say the team is always friendly, welcoming, professional and a real privilege to work with. Each title is the result of teamwork. The author produces a skeleton of words and photographs, but the Cicerone team gives it body and clothing fit for the outdoors.

In 2008, Hazel eloped to sail the canals of France on a rather small boat. Lois Sparling stepped in to the role with a whole new set of skills for the digital age. A highly experienced editor and with tremendous energy, Lois brought real sharpness to editorial and production processes and led the digital transformation of Cicerone to ensure that edited guides move seamlessly into production and that all guides are available electronically in various formats.

In the summer of 2008 (the year of the financial crash), Jonathan and Lesley had been trekking in the Alps, first in the Vanoise National Park, then across the border in the Gran Paradiso region of Italy. A few weeks later, business brought Jonathan down south, where he strayed into Kent and spent a few days with author Kev Reynolds and his wife to discuss various book projects. It was then that the financial world went into free fall with the collapse of several major banks. It was a time of great anxiety and uncertainty, but publisher and author went walking to clear their heads of gloom, and as they walked they reminisced about epic treks they'd tackled, either separately or together, then began to devise a book that would describe 20 major treks in the European Alps. It would include well-known routes such as the Tour of Mont Blanc and the Chamonix to Zermatt Walker's Haute Route, as well as little-known treks like those tackled by Jonathan and Lesley earlier that summer in the Vanoise and Gran Paradiso.

By the time they returned to the Reynolds' cottage, they had a list of 20 routes and the authors to write them. So, while countless other business leaders were biting their nails and holding their breath, Cicerone was committing a sizeable chunk of its money to the production of *Trekking in the Alps*, demonstrating faith in the future and determination to continue the company's tradition of providing for its readers 'a great day out on the hill'.

That tradition had begun with Walt and Brian. It was picked up by Jonathan and Lesley and remains at the very heart of the business. 'A great day out on the hill' – or on the trail, whether on foot, by bike or on skis – is what it's all about. All those who work for Cicerone are active outdoor people. Jonathan and Lesley escape to the hills and trails whenever they can; son Joe is a rock climber, mountaineer, trekker and fell runner; daughter Madeline has trekked several major routes in the Alps, and 'horse-trekked' in Kyrgyzstan's Tian Shan mountains, Morocco and Namibia.

In 2016, Lois stepped down after eight years as editorial manager, having recruited experienced editor Andrea Grimshaw as her successor. Like Lois, Andrea had copy-edited many Cicerone guides before joining the office team so she knew (or should have known) what she was getting into!

And so to 2017, by which time the business had outgrown Police Square in Milnthorpe. Having been converted from two old cottages, the Milnthorpe office had always had its own set of challenges beyond those of book production. In winter, those who worked downstairs would need to wear fleeces to keep warm, while those in the production room would bask in the relative warmth created by the server and four large computers. In summer, the comfort was reversed as those downstairs remained moderately cool, while the upstairs folk would wilt. At such times there'd be a call for ice cream. At other times there'd be cake. Cicerone is fuelled by cake. Cake for birthdays. Cake to mark an anniversary. Cake because it's Friday. Any occasion – or none at all – is celebrated with cake.

So in 2017, having found a modern, purpose-built office space on the edge of Kendal, the Cicerone 'family' unplugged their computers and moved into their new home. The aptly named Juniper House was ideal, with open airy spaces and room to expand. It was a big bite, but it was worth it. And it would, of course, be just a bit closer to the hills...

It is to the hills, the mountains and the countryside at its best that Cicerone's focus and the attention of its authors continues to be directed. The earliest guides were to the Lakes and Scotland, and 50 years on, the list of titles covering these areas has grown considerably. But horizons have been stretched, and today's catalogue also includes guides to a great range of exciting destinations, including the Alps and Andalucía, Bhutan and the Balkans, Patagonia and Peru, Norway and Nepal and the trek to Everest Base Camp. As this book goes to print, there will be Cicerone authors at work in various far-flung corners of the globe, having adventures, researching new routes, no doubt getting lost (so that their readers won't) and devising ways to turn dreams into reality. That's what guidebooks are all about: creating dreams, feeding them and making them come true.

> "'A great day out on the hill" ...is what it's all about'

Over Cicerone's lifetime, the environment around the publishing industry has changed out of all recognition. From small independent book stores to chain stores and Amazon, from hand-crafted pages and hot metal to modern publishing technology, from local printers to the Far East, and now digital printing, the growth and eclipse and now hopefully the recovery of independent stores, from the pen to the e-book, from the library to the internet, mobile computers and artificial intelligence, from handmade maps to digital maps on phones, from ferries and currency limits to low-cost airlines and credit cards, from the strikes of the 1970s through Thatcherism and austerity again, from joining the EU to leaving it, from controlled pricing of books to survival of the biggest.

Despite all this change, the essentials are unaffected. Cicerone's mission is still to provide the inspiration, essential information and guidance for adventures 'out there'. As Jonathan says, 'our job, our purpose, is to provide a great time on the hill' – or on the trail, trek or climb.

Kev Reynolds, with Jonathan Williams

Fifty years – A TIMELINE

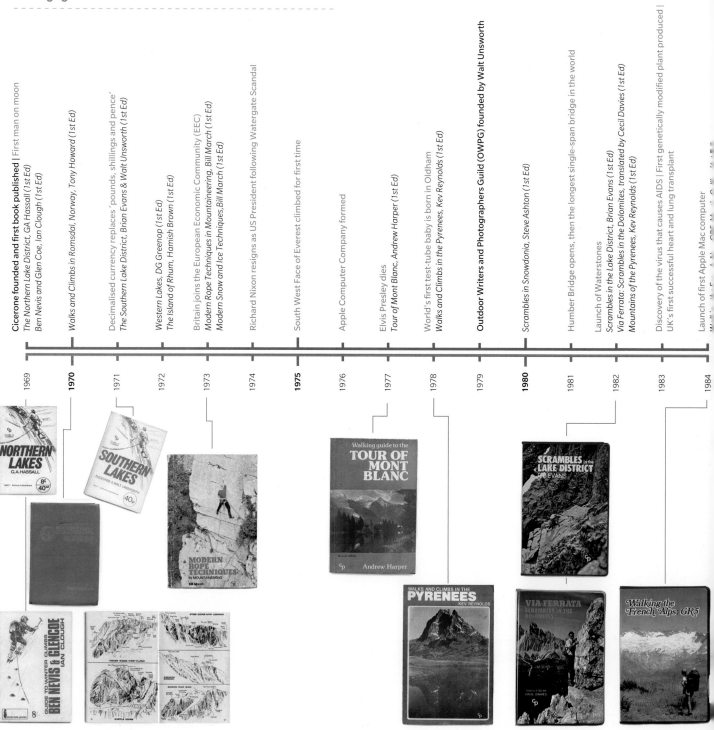

Cicerone founded and first book published | First man on moon
The Northern Lake District, GA Hassall (1st Ed)
Ben Nevis and Glen Coe, Ian Clough (1st Ed)

Walks and Climbs in Romsdal, Norway, Tony Howard (1st Ed)

Decimalised currency replaces 'pounds, shillings and pence'
The Southern Lake District, Brian Evans & Walt Unsworth (1st Ed)

Western Lakes, DG Greenop (1st Ed)
The Island of Rhum, Hamish Brown (1st Ed)

Britain joins the European Economic Community (EEC)
Modern Rope Techniques in Mountaineering, Bill March (1st Ed)
Modern Snow and Ice Techniques, Bill March (1st Ed)

Richard Nixon resigns as US President following Watergate Scandal

South West Face of Everest climbed for first time

Apple Computer Company formed

Elvis Presley dies
Tour of Mont Blanc, Andrew Harper (1st Ed)

World's first test-tube baby is born in Oldham
Walks and Climbs in the Pyrenees, Kev Reynolds (1st Ed)

Outdoor Writers and Photographers Guild (OWPG) founded by Walt Unsworth

Scrambles in Snowdonia, Steve Ashton (1st Ed)

Humber Bridge opens, then the longest single-span bridge in the world

Launch of Waterstones
Scrambles in the Lake District, Brian Evans (1st Ed)
Via Ferrata: Scrambles in the Dolomites, translated by Cecil Davies (1st Ed)
Mountains of the Pyrenees, Kev Reynolds (1st Ed)

Discovery of the virus that causes AIDS | First genetically modified plant produced |
UK's first successful heart and lung transplant

Launch of first Apple Mac computer

| 1969 | **1970** | 1971 | 1972 | 1973 | 1974 | **1975** | 1976 | 1977 | 1978 | 1979 | **1980** | 1981 | 1982 | 1983 | 1984 |

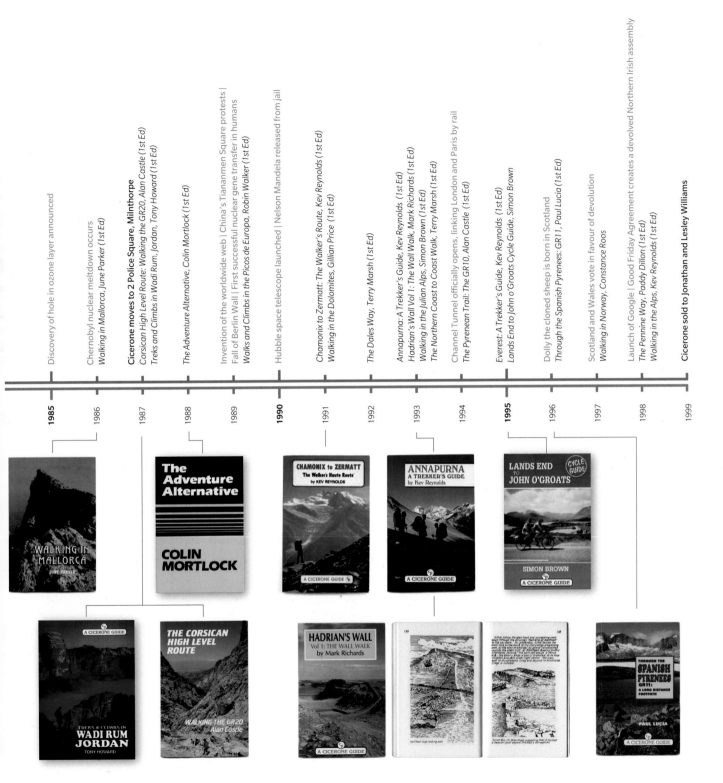

Discovery of hole in ozone layer announced

Chernobyl nuclear meltdown occurs
Walking in Mallorca, June Parker (1st Ed)

Cicerone moves to 2 Police Square, Milnthorpe
Corsican High Level Route: Walking the GR20, Alan Castle (1st Ed)
Treks and Climbs in Wadi Rum, Jordan, Tony Howard (1st Ed)

The Adventure Alternative, Colin Mortlock (1st Ed)

Invention of the worldwide web | China's Tiananmen Square protests |
Fall of Berlin Wall | First successful nuclear gene transfer in humans
Walks and Climbs in the Picos de Europa, Robin Walker (1st Ed)

Hubble space telescope launched | Nelson Mandela released from jail

Chamonix to Zermatt: The Walker's Route, Kev Reynolds (1st Ed)
Walking in the Dolomites, Gillian Price (1st Ed)

The Dales Way, Terry Marsh (1st Ed)

Annapurna: A Trekker's Guide, Kev Reynolds (1st Ed)
Hadrian's Wall Vol 1: The Wall Walk, Mark Richards (1st Ed)
Walking in the Julian Alps, Simon Brown (1st Ed)
The Northern Coast to Coast Walk, Terry Marsh (1st Ed)

Channel Tunnel officially opens, linking London and Paris by rail
The Pyrenean Trail: The GR10, Alan Castle (1st Ed)

Everest: A Trekker's Guide, Kev Reynolds (1st Ed)
Lands End to John o'Groats Cycle Guide, Simon Brown

Dolly the cloned sheep is born in Scotland
Through the Spanish Pyrenees: GR11, Paul Lucia (1st Ed)

Scotland and Wales vote in favour of devolution
Walking in Norway, Constance Roos

Launch of Google | Good Friday Agreement creates a devolved Northern Irish assembly
The Pennine Way, Paddy Dillon (1st Ed)
Walking in the Alps, Kev Reynolds (1st Ed)

Cicerone sold to Jonathan and Lesley Williams

1985 1986 1987 1988 1989 **1990** 1991 1992 1993 1994 **1995** 1996 1997 1998 1999

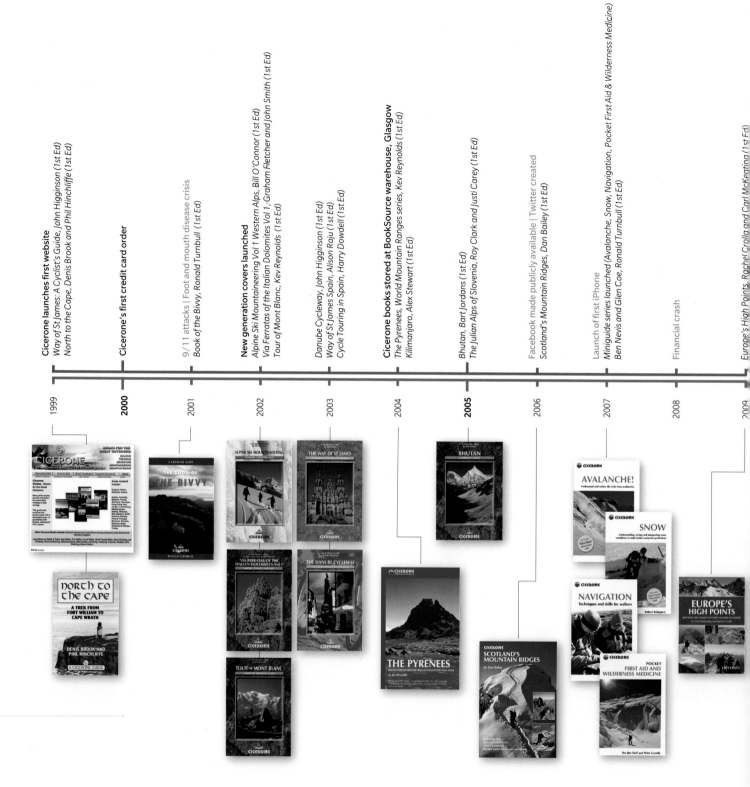

Cicerone launches first website
Way of St James: A Cyclist's Guide, John Higginson (1st Ed)
North to the Cape, Denis Brook and Phil Hinchliffe (1st Ed)

Cicerone's first credit card order

9/11 attacks | Foot and mouth disease crisis
Book of the Bivvy, Ronald Turnbull (1st Ed)

New generation covers launched
Alpine Ski Mountaineering Vol 1 Western Alps, Bill O'Connor (1st Ed)
Via Ferratas of the Italian Dolomites Vol 1; Graham Fletcher and John Smith (1st Ed)
Tour of Mont Blanc, Kev Reynolds (1st Ed)

Danube Cycleway, John Higginson (1st Ed)
Way of St James Spain, Alison Raju (1st Ed)
Cycle Touring in Spain, Harry Dowdell (1st Ed)

Cicerone books stored at BookSource warehouse, Glasgow
The Pyrenees, World Mountain Ranges series, Kev Reynolds (1st Ed)
Kilimanjaro, Alex Stewart (1st Ed)

Bhutan, Bart Jordans (1st Ed)
The Julian Alps of Slovenia, Roy Clark and Justi Carey (1st Ed)

Facebook made publicly available | Twitter created
Scotland's Mountain Ridges, Dan Bailey (1st Ed)

Launch of first iPhone
Miniguide series launched (Avalanche, Snow, Navigation, Pocket First Aid & Wilderness Medicine)
Ben Nevis and Glen Coe, Ronald Turnbull (1st Ed)

Financial crash

Europe's High Points, Rachel Crolla and Carl McKeating (1st Ed)

1999   **2000**   2001   2002   2003   2004   **2005**   2006   2007   2008   2009

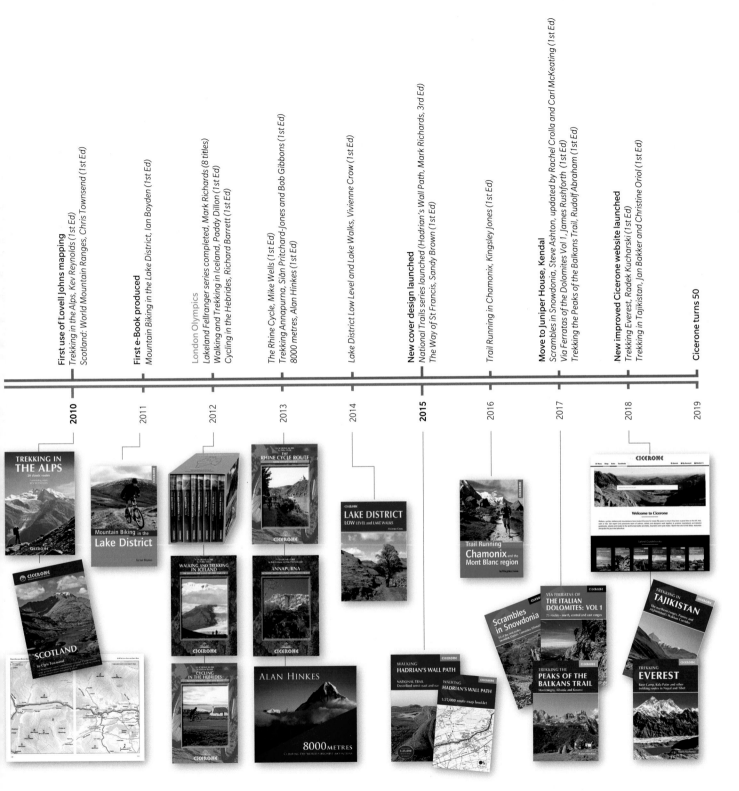

First use of Lovell Johns mapping
Trekking in the Alps, Kev Reynolds (1st Ed)
Scotland: World Mountain Ranges, Chris Townsend (1st Ed)

First e-Book produced
Mountain Biking in the Lake District, Ian Boyden (1st Ed)

London Olympics
Lakeland Fellranger series completed, Mark Richards (8 titles)
Walking and Trekking in Iceland, Paddy Dillon (1st Ed)
Cycling in the Hebrides, Richard Barrett (1st Ed)

The Rhine Cycle, Mike Wells (1st Ed)
Trekking Annapurna, Siân Pritchard-Jones and Bob Gibbons (1st Ed)
8000 metres, Alan Hinkes (1st Ed)

Lake District Low Level and Lake Walks, Vivienne Crow (1st Ed)

New cover design launched
National Trails series launched (Hadrian's Wall Path, Mark Richards, 3rd Ed)
The Way of St Francis, Sandy Brown (1st Ed)

Trail Running in Chamonix, Kingsley Jones (1st Ed)

Move to Juniper House, Kendal
Scrambles in Snowdonia, Steve Ashton, updated by Rachel Crolla and Carl McKeating (1st Ed)
Via Ferratas of the Dolomites Vol 1, James Rushforth (1st Ed)
Trekking the Peaks of the Balkans Trail, Rudolf Abraham (1st Ed)

New improved Cicerone website launched
Trekking Everest, Radek Kucharski (1st Ed)
Trekking in Tajikistan, Jan Bakker and Christine Oriol (1st Ed)

Cicerone turns 50

2010 2011 2012 2013 2014 **2015** 2016 2017 2018 2019

ORKNEY
ISLANDS

SHETLAND
ISLANDS

Ben Hope ▲

Ben More Assynt ▲

An Teallach ▲ ▲ Beinn Dearg

Beinn Eighe ▲

ISLE
OF SKYE

Ben Macdui ▲
Ben
Nevis ▲   SCOTLAND

Ben Lawers ▲

ATLANTIC OCEAN

Ben
Lomond ▲

Edinburgh ○

Glasgow ○

Southern Uplands

Cheviot
Hills

NORTH SEA

UNITED
KINGDOM

NORTHERN
IRELAND

Belfast ○

Scafell
Pike ▲

ISLE
OF MAN

Ingleborough ▲

Slieve
Donard ▲

IRISH SEA

Dublin ○

IRELAND

Kinder
Scout ▲

Lugnaquilla ▲

Snowdon ▲

ENGLAND

Cadair Idris ▲

Carrauntoohil ▲

WALES

Pen y Fan ▲
Cardiff ○

London ○

ENGLISH CHANNEL

Out there
ADVENTURES IN THE UK

Collins English Dictionary defines an adventure as 'a risky undertaking, the ending of which is uncertain'. Dictionary.com describes it as 'an exciting or very unusual experience' and 'participation in exciting undertakings'. Some of the 'adventures' described in this book are indeed risky undertakings, but not all of them. Some undoubtedly had uncertain endings – extreme adventures, with death or serious injury a distinct possibility; others are about the excitement of unusual experiences, where the 'adventurer' has stepped outside the comfort zone of home life, and simply gone wandering, not knowing how the day will pan out or where it will take them. That is what Cicerone is about: adventure in its broadest sense, steering readers towards a day, a week, or a whole month or two in which to celebrate the joy of being 'out there'.

In this section, our authors find their own definitions of adventure among the Highlands and Southern Uplands of Scotland; in the Lakes, the Dales and the Peak District, and in the coastal beauty of the Isle of Man; on the Pennine Way and the airy ridges of Snowdonia; in the Welsh borderlands and in the gentle lowlands of southern England. They travel by bike; they walk, they run, they climb, they scramble and they sleep in amazing places, for adventure is in their blood.

1 Walk on the wild side

PHOEBE SMITH

'The stripper's arrived!'

It's not a phrase you would imagine hearing on entering one of Scotland's mountain huts – especially one as remote as Glencoul in the north-west Highlands. But as I approached the green door of this little bothy, after struggling through a particularly difficult river crossing, it was the cry that greeted me.

It seems I had unwittingly crashed a stag party.

Making up one of the 100-strong network of abandoned old buildings looked after by the Mountain Bothies Association for walkers and climbers to sleep in free of charge, Glencoul is a former family home, abandoned in the 1950s, perched on the edge of the loch from which it gets its name. The nearest settlement is the tiny fishing hamlet of Kylesku, around an hour's drive from the northern town of Ullapool.

After battling hail and gale force winds, then tackling the burn, in spate, to get there, company was something I hadn't banked on. For a couple of seconds I was worried. In all my adventures exploring the UK, was this to be the bothy stay where it all went terribly wrong? There was only one way to find out. So, with a deep breath, I pushed open the door.

'I had unwittingly crashed a stag party'

Immediately I was met with warm smiles, offered the seat right next to the fire, given dry clothes to change into and fed hot food. It turned out this merry band of bachelors had arrived via fishing boat to give their friend a wild send-off (of the less raucous kind) before his 'big day'.

We talked for hours – of secret Scottish sleeping spots, magnificent mountain memories and some of the best bothy stays we'd ever had. When they asked me about my best, I said I'd tell them in the morning.

That night, they cleared out one of the two rooms in this, the former estate's schoolhouse, so I would have my own space. Then, as dawn broke, they woke me with a plate of pancakes, blueberries and cream, and absolutely insisted I accompany them on the boat back to Kylesku.

It just goes to show that first impressions can often be proved wrong, that the wilderness can bring out the very best in people and that serendipity is a truly wonderful thing.

As we took the little vessel back across the loch in the driving rain, one of them asked me again which bothy experience had been the best. I smiled and said, 'the one where I ended up joining a stag party and spending the evening with some of the dearest people I could have ever hoped to meet'.

2 Glen Sligachan

TERRY MARSH

In 1973, in persistent rainfall, I perched beside the lapping waters of Loch na Crèitheach in Glen Sligachan on Skye eating a tin of mandarin oranges. It was bliss, yet bizarre, a moment filled with the contentment that comes from knowing you're doing something a bit eccentric, but which adds to life's experience.

Of course, there are many great walking opportunities on Skye, but for unadulterated grandeur, nothing quite rouses the passions like this great glen, a rough divide between the Black Cuillin and the Red – a masterpiece of nature's handiwork.

On a gloomy day, the glen, viewed from Sligachan, looks like a thinly disguised highway to hell. On that first visit I was on my own and a little apprehensive, born of the glen's dark reputation, but determined to investigate for myself. Since then I've repeated the walk many times, often including the diversion over the Sgùrr Hain ridge to Coruisk and the infamous Bad Step.

In 2012, I was with my son and grandson; the blue sky was pierced by sharply etched crags, and there was enough of a breeze to keep the midges at bay. The dome of Glamaig was soon behind us and we slipped on below the pyramid of Marsco, to the north-east of which Bonnie Prince Charlie passed on his escape, bound for France.

'For unadulterated grandeur, nothing quite rouses the passions like this great glen'

As we moved into the glen, the view of Sgùrr nan Gillean now embraced the renowned Pinnacle Ridge, a heady dose of heavy-duty scrambling, not seen in profile until this point. Ahead, two low-lying lochans eventually came into view: the Black Lochs. One feeds north into the River Sligachan, which here curves down from the dark recesses of Harta Corrie; the other flows southwards, effectively marking the watershed of the walk, reached after 6km of walking.

Beyond Loch an Athain, we ambled into Srath na Crèitheach, a wide glen that crosses the base of Blà Bheinn (Blaven), a Black Cuillin outlier. For a moment, the skies darkened, threatening rain, but beyond Loch na Crèitheach we burst out into the unexpected-if-you're-not-expecting-it sandy, and sunny, expanse of Camasunary.

Here, Glen Sligachan comes to an end. We explored the bothy, had a second round of lunch in the company of oystercatcher, sandpiper, ringed plover and, out in the bay, great northern diver, then escaped eastwards by a broad track up to the Bealach Am Màm. It's a great vantage point, putting the whole Cuillin ridge on view. We talked of continuing to Elgol, as many do, but the glen was what the day had been all about. Elgol would have been one brushstroke too many on this particular canvas.

▼ Sgùrr nan Gillean at the entrance to Glen Sligachan (photo: Terry Marsh)

▲ Ben Nevis (left) and Càrn Mòr Dearg – the East Ridge runs along the line of light and shadow (photo: Dan Bailey)

3 The Lochaber Traverse

DAN BAILEY

Morning had barely begun, but what a day it promised to be: white-crusted peaks poking out of dense fog beneath an empty blue sky, windless and T-shirt-warm in the sun. Ben Nevis summit experiences are rarely this idyllic, and I felt no urge to hurry. But I had plenty yet to do, and the promise of great things ahead spurred me on.

Treading the roof of the West Highlands along the Grey Corries and over Aonach Beag and Aonach Mòr, and finishing with a flourish on the Càrn Mòr Dearg Arête and Ben Nevis, the Lochaber Traverse is the ultimate Scottish high-altitude hillwalk, and arguably the grandest route in Britain available to the averagely fit and competent. With four 4000-footers, the highest point in the UK, some dramatic (easy) scrambling and about 3000m ascent over roughly 25km of continuously memorable ridge walking, this trip does not suit understatement.

In snow, the walk dips a toe into real mountaineering. On two previous traverses, I'd failed to strike the magic combination of wintry conditions and fine weather, but now I'd really hit the jackpot. This time I started with the Ben. Although counter-intuitive, a west-to-east crossing winds slowly down all the way from this high point, and also provides the chance to kick off in style with a dawn ascent of Ledge Route, a classic climb through the grandeur of the mountain's northern crags.

Down now to the CMD Arête, that perfect curving walkway hitched onto the flank of Ben Nevis. Part snow and part rock, its blocky crest proved as enjoyably airy as ever, while the view of the Ben's complex crags slowly unrolled across Coire Leis. Up on Càrn Mòr Dearg, I left the trodden trail behind. Easier on paper than the CMD Arête, but today less straightforward on the ground, the wind-honed snow crest of the East Ridge had turned to precarious slush in the sun. By now I'd come to resent the redundant winter layers that bulked my pack. But when you're wearing shades and sun-cream in Scotland, in March, you can forgive a lot.

On the domed summit of Aonach Beag, a familiar brimmed hat descended over the brow towards me. Attached to it was outdoor writing colleague Alex Roddie, on his own east–west traverse. He looked quietly ecstatic, blown away by the sheer perfection of this route, in these conditions. I'm sure I wore an identical expression. With an exchange of hints on the tricky bits to come, we set off in each other's footsteps – for my part strangely cheered by this shared moment in a place so breathtakingly big.

> 'The CMD Arête, that perfect curving walkway hitched onto the flank of Ben Nevis'

4 Climbing Orion Direct

MIKE PESCOD

Climbing Orion Direct on Ben Nevis on a sunny day is usually a once-in-a-lifetime experience. Working as a mountain guide based in Fort William, I am lucky enough to enjoy the experience of this amazing route time and time again. Added to this is the enjoyment of making it possible for other people to achieve something on their bucket list, which gives another level of satisfaction to the climb.

As you walk up the Allt a'Mhuilinn, like the faithful on a pilgrimage, the Orion Face stands directly in front of you. It is the biggest face on Ben Nevis, one of the biggest ice climbs in the country, and uniquely Scottish. Only the right combination of snowfall, thaw and refreeze, a cycle repeated many times in many storms throughout the dark months of winter, will cover the face in snow-ice. This snow-ice is sufficiently solid to climb but rarely satisfactory for protecting the route. Ice screws will, at best, be spaced, and sometimes placed for decoration rather than for effectiveness. And there are eight or nine long, intricate pitches to reach the top.

The route is a non-line that shows the brilliant mountaineering skill of the first ascensionists. It links natural features, which are not obvious from the bottom, in a devious line that makes perfect sense. The pitches flow together with sustained climbing that is always delicate but never hard. Despite not having an obvious line like Point Five Gully, it has an aesthetic all to itself.

> 'One of the biggest ice climbs in the country, and uniquely Scottish'

Every time I climb Orion Direct, I tell the people I'm with about its first ascent in 1960 by Jimmy Marshall and Robin Smith, with one ice axe each and a single rope. This was at the end of a week of climbing that has become legendary, the pinnacle of the step-cutting era. Every day for six days, Marshall and Smith climbed a new route at the highest standard of the time, before taking a day off. This they spent walking over Càrn Mòr Dearg, Aonach Beag and the Grey Corries to Spean Bridge.

Orion Direct was their last climb of the week. Just imagine setting off up this 400m face of ice and rock knowing that the only way off was to reach the top! Thankfully we have modern equipment nowadays to make the climb a little more accessible and less serious. However, for those who climb it, it will never lose any of its impact.

▽ John Gilbert climbing Orion Direct in February 2018 (photo: Mike Pescod)

5 Loch Enoch

RONALD TURNBULL

The Southern Uplands. Over 100 separate summits. Hart Fell, with its Beeftub hollow and the grassy swoop of Saddle Yoke. White Coomb, with its Grey Mare's waterfall. Distant Cheviot with its Hen Hole. Mighty Merrick, with its fabled view (on a very, very clear day) of Snowdon beyond the Isle of Man.

And yet in all this 200km of hill range, stretching coast to coast, the one walk to keep coming back to isn't a summit at all. It's Loch Enoch, half a day's walk from anywhere, in a wilderness of black peat and yellow autumn grasses and bare grey granite. You'll find it on the 500m contour in the hollow between the Hills of the Dungeon and the Range of the Awful Hand.

You start from Loch Trool, where a granite boulder's been remounted as a memorial to a minor victory in Robert the Bruce's war of independence. Through an oak wood and over an old stone bridge, the path leads up between the hills to a higher loch, Loch Valley. The path's a mess of peat and boulders, but the loch is lovely, between knobby slopes of grass and bare rock.

Continue past waterfalls and a lonely rowan to a third loch, called Neldricken. A corner of it, surrounded by rushes and full of grey water,

'Between the Hills of the Dungeon and the Range of the Awful Hand'

is known as the Murder Hole. Here, the vile Macaterick clan murdered passing hillwalkers, stole our lovely Gore-Tex jackets and tramped our bodies into the peat – depending on which history you read. The path gets smaller, hops across a stream, and heads up towards what looks like nowhere at all – but is actually Loch Enoch.

Loch Enoch sprawls like an amoeba across two or three square kilometres of granite bedrock. Its little beaches are silver granite sand. That sand is pure quartz, the crystals still sharp, so that it was once gathered to make into whetstones for scythes. The loch itself is bottomless, it never freezes over, and the largest of its islands contains a small peat pool, the Loch in the Loch. The first of those statements is unlikely and the second is untrue, for I have crossed the ice of Loch Enoch to visit that island with its lochan. It's also possible to swim Loch Enoch to the island. The Loch in the Loch is reported as pleasantly warm on a summer's day, but the swim back will quickly cool you down again.

Rarely have I met anyone at Loch Enoch. But one late spring morning I heard a gentle honking call. Two barnacle geese had found it the perfect pause on their migratory flight northwards.

Loch Enoch: it's the motorway pull-off on the way to Spitsbergen.

▼ Loch Enoch from Redstone Rig (photo: Ronald Turnbull)

> The south face of Great Gable

> Napes Needle – the classic view
> (artwork: Mark Richards)

6 A truly great mountain day

MARK RICHARDS

Sometimes everything comes together in the most wonderful way.

I have vivid recall of just such a kaleidoscope of adventure and fulfilment during a late summer expedition when I was intent on a bold ascent of Great Gable. Leaving home at first light, I travelled down the Eden Valley, pausing briefly on the A6 to admire and photograph a vintage Ferguson tractor marking out a pasture in preparation for ploughing. It was a moment of pure nostalgia, transporting me back to my farming roots. The sky was blue and remained so the entire day, although thankfully it was not too hot.

Parking at Seathwaite Farm, the road end at the head of Borrowdale, I climbed the age-old track to crest Styhead Pass. How fortunate we are that this wild corridor never became a tarmacked road, as was once contemplated. The common way up Great Gable from this spot is the Breast Route, but my mind was fixed on a greater adventure. So off I strode along the south traverse by Kern Knotts to dance across the screes spilling from Great Hell Gate and set foot on the lower ledges of the Great Napes.

Smartly climbing Needle Gully onto the Dress Circle, I was able to exchange a happy conversation with two climbers engaged on the classic Haskett-Smith route on Napes Needle. Now well off a path of any form, I angled left, going down an awkward mossy chimney then up again to the Sphinx Rock. Being alone, I didn't fancy the Sphinx Ridge direct, so clambered down into the stone shoot of Little Hell Gate, jerking upward to find far more inviting handholds on the upper section of the Sphinx Ridge to reach Tophet Bastion. I well remember the startled glare of three Herdwicks as they raised their heads from nibbling about the only blades of grass to be found on this ferocious slope.

'I felt as if I was standing on the roof of the world'

Westmorland Crags loomed but were easily rounded, after which I made it first to Westmorland Cairn and then the summit. There was not a soul in sight. Consumed by a wonderful feeling of completeness, for that one moment I felt as if I was standing on the roof of the world. It was the synthesis of what has always driven me to be an outdoor writer, and a delicious elation streamed through my veins.

37

7 Intake Ridge

BRIAN EVANS

Eccentric schoolteacher Bentley Beetham first climbed the ridge in 1937, looking for easy climbs on which to take his boys. Located at the entrance to Borrowdale's side valley, Combe Gill, it is hardly a continuous climb, more a succession of loosely connected rock ribs, now a popular scramble with a network of variations to suit every grade.

What makes it special is a smooth, glaciated grey dome, like a professor's head, the culmination of the first section. The scrambler is enticed by easy rocks to an airy platform below the dome, where the most exciting exit is to gain the crest by exposed slabs on small holds. 'Easier than it looks', I commented in my guidebook, but opinion seems to contest that impression. I am sure my advice to use a rope for protection was sound.

It is one small piece of a mountaineering day in Combe Gill, for the rocks of Intake Ridge can be linked almost to Bessyboot's pyramid top, then a descent to Dove's Nest Crag allows a visit to Attic Cave and another scramble up the crag's right side. I delight in caressing the solid knobbles of the easy slabs above, lingering on Combe Head and visually savouring the day's sport above the egg-basket moraines of the valley base.

> '**What makes it special is a smooth, glaciated grey dome, like a professor's head**'

So when Cicerone asked for a square-format photo for the new 2016 edition of my book, I immediately thought of Intake Ridge for a photo shoot.

Aileen and I had done little scrambling for years, enjoying other mountain adventures, so the preliminary rocks seemed more demanding, especially when looking up to the steep base of the dome – after all, we were well advanced in age! The airy platform seemed extremely exposed so we took the easier way up a steep crack, then delicately padded up the easing forehead of the dome, confidence and exhilaration returning.

Aileen's role was now as photographer, ensconced on the adjacent fellside, while I returned to the platform and romped up the rocks, enjoying every minute, relishing the feel of rough Borrowdale volcanic with its comforting texture and the positive grip of a small edge. Again and again I scrambled the dome, pausing to check Aileen's photos, then deciding 'just another one' – an excuse to prolong the enjoyment.

Satisfied at last, we dropped away from the rocks, collected patient collie Jess, tail windmilling in excitement, and headed home.

8 Running the Bob Graham Round

JOE WILLIAMS

The lightning illuminates the sky to the south, followed soon after by a thunder crash. I scream at my friends over the immense noise of the wind and hail – we're really in a storm now! I can't quite believe that the weather is this bad on the day of my Bob Graham Round attempt. But it is, and we are now approaching Helvellyn, the 11th peak on the 100km, 42-peak, 24-hour Lake District fell running challenge.

Some time later, we are on the climb up the steep slopes of Yewbarrow, and I work hard to keep up with my pacers. Fifteen hours in and I am breathing heavily, pulling on my poles and feeling the burn in my legs. The mysterious knee pain I've lived with while running over the Langdale and Scafell ranges has suddenly disappeared, the weather is changing from rainy to fine, and I'm with friends old and new.

After Yewbarrow, we stride up Red Pike, around Scoat Fell, onto Steeple and up Pillar. Rob and Steve take me on lines I've never considered venturing on before – fell runners' routes often devoid of path, but always the fastest way. After a lifetime of walking and climbing, I thought I knew the secrets of the mountains, but fell running has taught me far more. I know where the sheep travel, I understand the geology

'...time spent with friends and family among mountains I love'

and vegetation, and I can see more clearly the human impact on the fells. With fell running, I feel closer to the mountains and more comfortable in them.

One friend appears loyally every 15 minutes to feed me, and at every change from uphill to flat she carries my trekking poles when I run. Another is always ahead (I can never catch up with him, no matter how hard I try), scouting the route and navigating. The third never leaves my side, keeping a close eye on my steps, my running line – just being right there. Before Gable, another friend resupplies us with water (we don't break step), and we are joined by my dog, who leads the way up the rocks of Great Gable with a grand smile on her face.

The joy of the BG for me was in time spent with friends and family among mountains I love. Somehow this selfish endeavour of running around the Lake District feels meaningful and important. Thank you to those who joined me on my adventure.

▽ The support team – all those who helped me on the Bob Graham Round (photo: Joe Williams)

9 Bivvybag

RONALD TURNBULL

I could have written about almost a hundred hilltop bivvies: nights on soft heather, warm in an eiderdown bag, while the stars make great circles over my nose and daylight creeps up behind some interesting scenery such as Cornwall or the Cairngorms.

But Adventure is when you don't know how it's going to turn out – and it actually turns out nasty.

January's when the Lake District pretends to be somewhere in Scotland by emptying all the car parks and covering up the paths. After a rough night in the camping barn at Buttermere, I passed the lake in the dark, enjoyed a soggy sunrise in Scarth Gap, and reached Wasdale Head in time for lunch – which is where it got interesting. Up on Scafell

Pike it was snowing, and the cloud was down. And it was going to get dark in just four hours.

The north face route up Scafell Pike is knee-deep snow, so no worries about slipping off the hill. That's good, as the snow is quite steep between the scraps of crag that come and go in the mist. The plateau is soft snow on boulders. Frozen fingers could drop the compass, and a dropped compass will be gone for good. But one compass bearing's enough to fix the wind, and the wind guides me across the boulders. I get to Mickledore with 20 minutes of daylight still in hand.

Soft snow on grassy slopes is the quickest descending there is. The lower I get, the cosier the night ahead will be. I get right down to the flat floor of Eskdale, and by torchlight find a cosy boulder to snuggle down behind.

The night that follows is like a work of classic 19th-century literature. It's quite interesting, in bits. But above all, it's long.

There are chilly bits, when the cloud breaks and stars gleam above the great black slush-spattered shape of Cam Crag. And there are less chilly bits when the cloud comes down and it's snowing. There's the intriguing realisation that even a well-chilled human being can thaw a well-frozen bit of Eskdale into a puddle. And the useful discovery that two sets of fleece and two full waterproofs aren't actually all that warm, while exceedingly uncomfortable to move about in. And the insight that if you zip yourself right inside a bivvybag, the odours of the previous 100 bivvybag nights make a cold miasma that's slightly like the 52nd chapter of *Moby-Dick*…

There's very little insulation in four inches of overnight snow. But do you really know Upper Eskdale until you've woken up there, half frozen, in slush and low cloud, and tried to eat some muesli?

'The night that follows is like a work of classic 19th-century literature'

The morning after – the River Esk and Cam Spout Crag (photo: Ronald Turnbull)

10 A walk with the gulls

AILEEN EVANS

What could be better? A sunny summer day, ice cream in hand, striding out of Port Erin on the west coast of the Isle of Man to summit three hills, their sides continually pounded by the fierce Atlantic waves that skirt Ireland to fashion the dramatic cliffs of this coastline.

Today all was quiet, but people were hurrying past. Had I fallen into a festival at Milner's Tower on Bradda Head? After all, the view from here had won photographic awards. No, all eyes were peering down into the bay, where a visiting basking shark, huge mouth agape, was gently cruising, oblivious to a couple of curious canoeists. Passing the tower, I tore my eyes from the view to the first summit, Bradda Hill.

The path narrowed, became steeper and led down to the lonely yet pretty Fleshwick Bay. Something black rose from the water and turned out to be a group of wet-suited divers, who slithered over the seaweed-covered rocks with difficulty to gain the beach. 'I'm coming back when the water warms up,' one moaned in my direction, as I prepared to climb up the rough and apparently trackless moor to gain the summit of Lhiattee ny Beinnee.

> 'A sudden flash of white wings as gulls soared overhead'

I was not lost. Signposts pointed ever upward until gradually emerging views along the coastline revealed the distant Mountains of Mourne tingeing the horizon. What a delight! Purple heather contrasted with the vivid yellow of the summer-flowering dwarf gorse, and there was a sudden flash of white wings as gulls soared overhead.

The descent to the Sloc was accompanied by an intermittent noise and the sight of two men lying prone on the very edge of the cliff.

It was not a rescue; they were flying their recently built model planes.

Off once again up the slopes of the highest summit, Cronk ny Arrey Laa (437m/1434ft). Bygone local widows had trodden this path, obliged to supply fuel for the beacon – and for the watchman, for the name translates as 'Hill of the Morning Watch'. This 360-degree vantage point would have been an excellent place from which to watch for Napoleon, but he didn't come. From the huge cairn at the summit, I, however, was able to spy out my destination, via the beautiful White Beach to the tail of rocks at Niarbyl and a cup of tea at the Manx National Heritage café.

▼ On the Isle of Man coast path (photo: Aileen Evans)

11 The Bowderdale Classic

IAN BOYDON

It is easy to find remoteness and a quiet corner of the Dales to yourself, even during the height of summer – much easier than in the nearby Lake District, which can be all too often overrun with visitors, particularly at weekends. For the mountain bike adventurer seeking high altitude and big mountain views, but some semblance of solitude, a great option is a long tour of those often overlooked fells that lie just to the north of Sedbergh.

And so it was on one of those days when the weather was favourable for a high-level adventure that my good friend Kieran and I arrived in Sedbergh to take in one of the classic Dales mountain bike tours – a grand tour of the Howgills.

Following a brief tarmac ride out of town, we soon faced the incredibly steep climb up the flank of Winder. The first section is an inescapable push of around ten minutes, but after this, providing the fitness is there, the rest can be climbed in the saddle – albeit on the very nose of the saddle, and with a slice of luck.

Luck was on our side and, after a short recovery snack, we were soon enjoying an undulating high-altitude cruise across the tops of the Howgills, before a final push took us to the summit of the Calf. We hardly spied another soul, and the views, although slightly curtailed by the heat haze that is common in the northern summer months, were still panoramic and took the edge off aching legs.

However, the highlight of the route was yet to come – a steep and rocky plunge into the deserted valley of Bowderdale. Once in the valley, we picked our way along the sinuous and boulder-strewn singletrack above the stream that babbles below to the right.

After around an hour of riding north, we emerged from the valley and headed east to Ravenstonedale, where we enjoyed a cold drink in an inviting beer garden before heading south again to make the return trip.

Although the second half of the journey is not quite as spectacular as the first, it still packs in many wonderful highlights: we passed near the impressive Cautley Spout waterfalls, enjoyed narrow rooted descents through dense woodland and singletrack traverses of fellsides, and forded picturesque streams.

They may not have the glamour of their Lake District neighbours but, when it comes to mountain bike adventures, the Howgills are second to none.

⌃ Enjoying some singletrack biking in the Howgills (photo: Ian Boydon)

'An undulating high-altitude cruise across the tops of the Howgills'

▲ Gazing across East Grain to Simon's Seat
(photo: Dennis Kelsall)

12 Magic among the Howgills

DENNIS KELSALL

Monday night, camped at Ravenstonedale, held little promise, with blustery rain flapping the canvas and washing away any great enthusiasm for the following day's planned walk up the Calf. I dozed off, resigned to another day of waterproofs and the hope that a few 'atmospheric' cloud pictures might appease my editor. But next morning, as Morpheus relinquished his hold, I sensed change: hardly a breath of wind, an encouraging glow and the chatter of early morning birdsong. I peered out to a splendid autumnal dawn, a gentle dusting of hoar and barely a wisp of cloud. Downing porridge and coffee on the move, Jan and I were ready to go in record time.

A single car at Bowderdale suggested someone already ahead, but there was no sign of them as we strode the still-puddled track past rough intake enclosures into the long valley beyond. Below, the beck squirmed within the narrow flatness of the valley, fed by innumerable crystal springs seeping from the heights, while the steep, enclosing slopes focused our gaze towards the distant snout of Yarlside sundering the valley head. The only signs of life were a couple of Howgill

ponies, and a solitary heron optimistically searching the stream for a late breakfast.

The path seemed in little hurry to reach the tops, and 4 miles of gentle walking barely gained us 150m. The inevitable steepening came beyond Ram's Gill but, even here, the path took a well-considered curve above Hare Shaw and Swere Gill onto the ridge. The increasing height opened grand views across the dark crags of Cautley to Baugh and Wild Boar fells, an impressive backdrop during the final saunter to the top, where a shallow tarn laps incongruously beside the trig column.

Now sharing the still-glorious day with folk who had plodded up from Sedbergh, we wandered on over Bram Rigg Top, Calders and Great Dummacks for the dramatic view into Cautley. The vistas were stunning and, as we finished our soup, it was tempting to linger. But, with daylight hours set to dwindle, it was time to start back. We retraced our steps above Swere Gill to pick up the long, descending spur over Hazelgill Knott and West Fell. With Langdale and Bowderdale on either hand and a rich panorama ahead to Cross Fell, we could have asked for no finer sights to end the day.

13 The Pennine Way

PADDY DILLON

The Pennine Way was 30 years in the making, but when it opened I was just a 7-year-old boy who wouldn't go for a walk without kicking up a tantrum and demanding ice cream. When I was 16, I shouldered a heavy pack full of all the wrong gear that I'd quite literally begged, borrowed and stolen, and walked the 6 miles from my house to where I could join the Pennine Way.

The plan was simple. Follow the Way from Lancashire to Cross Fell, cut across the Vale of Eden to the Lake District, then return home through the Yorkshire Dales. I had £17.33 in my pocket to feed me for a month and campsites cost 20p a night. Maths was never my strong point, but I soon learned to budget!

I was a boy when I left home, but after only a few days I became a man. I remember the moment clearly. I was scrambling across rock on Malham Cove when I heard a little boy shouting: 'Daddy, daddy, look at that man!'

He was pointing. People were looking. It turned out I was the one being pointed at, and everyone was looking at me. All of a sudden I was a man. The Pennine Way made a man of me!

I made every mistake a young and inexperienced backpacker could make while struggling along the Pennine Way, suffered the consequences, and resolved never to make the same mistakes again. By the time I headed for the Lake District, I was a wise and experienced backpacker, but still carrying all the wrong gear.

I have walked the Pennine Way time and time again and can never tire of it. Some parts I have walked so often that I've lost count. It's my personal 'Memory Lane', where I drift into wistfulness and recall my previous selves trekking along the same route, summer and winter, day and night. I marvel at how easily I would cover 30 miles a day and curl up in a sleeping bag on a slab of rock under the stars.

There was a time when people would ask if you were a keen walker and almost immediately enquire, 'Have you walked the Pennine Way?' Answer 'yes' and your hill cred went up, but answer 'no' and it was clear you weren't really a keen walker. That's no longer the case, but the Pennine Way remains a firm favourite with me.

'I had £17.33 in my
pocket to feed me for
a month'

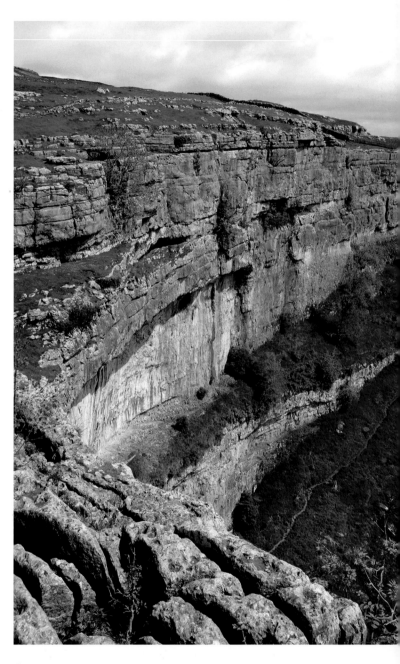

Rugged limestone pavements reach the edge of Malham Cove
(photo: Paddy Dillon)

45

14 The Tissington Trail

CHIZ DAKIN

If you step away from the frenetic traffic arteries between the busy towns and centres of attraction in the Peak District, a capillary network of quiet narrow country lanes emerges – perfect terrain for cycling. Then add exciting (but not overly technical) off-road terrain, café options and an easy return along a former railway line, and you're set for a fabulous adventure on a variety of surfaces perfect for a gravel bike.

It was a hot 'Indian summer' day when we started from the car park at Tissington. No easy line along the Trail for us yet though – we were beginning with a section of the 'Tour de Peak District' multi-day route, crossing unfenced high pasture and descending to the challenging Tissington Ford. But on a hot day with low water flow there was no need for the footbridge, and the gentle cooling splash gave us little cause for concern – unlike in winter conditions, when unsuspecting vehicles can be swept away!

We enjoyed the leafy shade of a tunnel of trees overhanging the road to Bradbourne, climbed through Brassington's narrow lanes past gritstone cottages to plateau height, then enjoyed a fast descent to Via Gellia. Although carrying a bendy major road, the steep-sided valley provided welcome cooling shade and a gentle ascent back towards Grangemill. (In spring, the pungent aroma of wild garlic pervades the valley.)

A steep ascent to Bonsall Moor became a dry corrugated track; near Winster, we peered into the former lead-mining 'safe house', where newly mined ore could be 'banked' overnight for safe keeping.

The gravel bike now showed its tougher side on a narrow and rocky descent to Elton. Then came quiet, chipping-edged lanes, steep undulations, the site of a now-invisible medieval village – all flowed fast to Middleton, where it was time for a well-earned café stop. Hot from the oven, freshly baked scones with clotted cream were perfect as we relaxed on sunny benches.

Freshly refuelled, we were ready for the steep ascent out of Middleton followed by an exciting off-road descent to the High Peak Trail. Potholes deteriorated into a challenging variety of loose rock, mud and ruts on a bouncy descent with a few testing bits of uphill. We were lucky it was so dry; after heavy rain, the muddy potholes quickly coalesce into an unhelpfully gloopy lane of puddles.

Finally, the Tissington Trail took us gently back to a refreshing ice cream – the perfect end to a thoroughly enjoyable ride!

> 'a capillary network of quiet narrow country lanes'

◀ Tissington Ford on a benign summer's day (photo: Chiz Dakin)

15 The secret side of Snowdon

RACHEL CROLLA

It had been a second great summer of camping with the family in the Ogwen Valley, where big blue skies dominated our days. Having two very young children, my hours spent in the mountains seemed precious and almost hedonistic, so my partner, Carl, and I took turns going scrambling, often accompanied by keen volunteers with whom we had struck up acquaintances.

So it was that I set off up Cwm Glas Mawr from the Llanberis Pass on the northern side of the Snowdon massif with Katie, a devoted fell runner turned scrambler for the day. As we followed the river steeply up the hillside, we could see our first objective – the slabby rocks barring the entrance to Cwm Glas. Conditions were perfect on the bone-dry slabs, so we took the harder option, relishing the short-lived technicality of the moves and then moving quickly up right of the watercourse to skirt the tiny secret waters of Llyn Bach.

Here, we felt secluded and far away from the hustle and bustle of the Snowdon Horseshoe and Crib y Ddysgl high above us. The next scramble – the Clogwyn y Person Arête – was starkly obvious and

'the spectacular pinnacles of the route had an unforgettable, almost magical quality'

the line was stunning, rising sharply from the truncating cliffs of the Parson's Nose. As with many scrambles, a variety of options existed. We chose to get out the rope and tackle the Parson's Nose head-on. I paused at its top on the sun-drenched rock, wanting to savour the moment; perched mid-scramble, we ate a late lunch and I chatted with ease with my new-found companion about life and adventure.

An exciting down-climb from the Nose led us onto the ridge proper, where the scrambling remained challenging and exhilarating. The Person Arête is the ideal link-up scramble, and that day, in the late afternoon breeze, we made the most of the ample rock as we continued across the airy traverse of Crib Goch. As one of the best-known scrambles in the UK, Crib Goch is always breathtaking but often busy. That day, we saw only one other person the whole time we were out, and the spectacular pinnacles of the route had an unforgettable, almost magical quality. With yet more scrambling to descend the mountain's East Ridge, it was one of those perfect mountain days.

The descent to Kington overlooks a broad panoramic view (photo: Mike Dunn)

16 Hergest Ridge

MIKE DUNN

We're on the great flat whalebone of Hergest Ridge in far west Herefordshire again, revelling in the walk along the summit plateau and drinking in the extraordinary views. It's the fourth time in as many months, but some places just keep drawing you back, demanding another visit. We're in good company: Mike Oldfield found it irresistible too, taking refuge here after the success of *Tubular Bells* overwhelmed him.

We start at Gladestry this time, the short sharp ascent of Broken Bank soon forgotten as we reach the long summit ridge. As usual, a kaleidoscope of sensations assails us, from the touch of our boots on shaly bedrock on the eroded upper reaches of Broken Bank to the subtle coconut scent of the gorse in flower and the sounds of birdsong – this time the plaintive cry of golden plovers wheeling above the common, rather than the fierce scolding of winter flocks of fieldfare flitting from bush to bush.

Our progress is fast and easy on springy turf on the summit ridge, the grass close-cropped not only from the attentions of sheep and groups of diminutive Welsh mountain ponies but also from the boots of Offa's Dyke Path walkers. Then we pause as an extraordinary panorama

'Some places just keep drawing you back, demanding another visit'

takes in the pale blue outline of the Black Mountains in the south, Radnor Forest and the hills of mid Wales to the west, and the Malvern Hills on the eastern horizon.

But Hergest Ridge is also a place to expect the unexpected. We cross the wide green track of Kington's old racecourse, a place of revelry in the Victorian era, then swing left to inspect the Whet Stone, perhaps the largest of the glacial erratics littering the ridge. These massive boulders were carried by ice from the adjacent Hanter Hill, an igneous intrusion formed from the oldest rocks in Wales. But crowning the highest point on the ridge is a wholly unexpected stand of monkey puzzle trees, wildly out of place but a useful landmark nonetheless.

Our descent leads gently down a broad green track with Kington and much of Herefordshire in sight ahead. One last detour takes us into Hergest Croft, the manor house allegedly haunted by the black dog of Hergest, its gardens famed for their rhododendrons, azaleas and specimen trees. And so into the border town of Kington, to celebrate one of the great walks of the Welsh borderlands in one of its great pubs, the intimate and historic Olde Tavern.

17 The Thames Path

LEIGH HATTS

Having walked the trail from the Thames Barrier to the source in Gloucestershire for 40 years and still excited by the changing countryside and river, I took a Londoner, who had often wondered where the water came from, on the long walk upstream.

Tea at the end of the first day was by the path in the refectory of Southwark Cathedral, known to Chaucer and Shakespeare, for we were on a journey of heritage as well as nature. In the gathering darkness, skyscrapers were lighting up the river as we pressed on past Shakespeare's Globe. Day 2 brought the Houses of Parliament and Syon water meadows, washed twice daily by the tide. The big surprise had been the new moated US Embassy at Nine Elms. But the great delight was, as always, how quickly an illusion of countryside envelopes London's river beyond Putney, while at Runnymede we marvelled at being alone on a vast sunlit meadow which has a resonance for so many who may never visit.

The best was yet to come, for beyond Oxford the contrast with the hard-surface London tourist path was pronounced. Only a few reach Bablock Hythe, where the pub has seasonal hours. Here, we were really on our own with no turning back, as my companion conceded that walking the path was an adventure to be appreciated.

We continued on our way feeling both awed and lonely as low mist hung over Northmoor, and were a little anxious as dusk fell, although the prospect of beds at Rectory Farm, at the end of an almost imperceptible inland causeway, or at the Rose Revived, beside Newbridge's old bridge, allowed us time to enjoy the sound of water without traffic.

Ahead lay unchanging Chimney, wooden Tenfoot Bridge, Tadpole Bridge and Rushey Lock. At Kelmscott, lunch was at the Plough alongside William Morris's house. Sailing to here from his Hammersmith home took him as long as it had taken us, for he too believed that lingering in ancient churches and inns was part of the experience.

Navigation end at Inglesham is no more than a round tower and a 13th-century church; as we sat, I told of Percy Bysshe Shelley's boat running into reeds here. Although the towpath also ends here, the trail is always being improved so we were able to continue on a newly opened waterside path.

It did not matter that the source was dry. The journey itself was both our achievement and our reward.

> 'Lingering in ancient churches and inns was part of the experience'

▽ St Paul's, seen across the river from the South Bank (photo: Leigh Hatts)

Out there
ADVENTURES IN EUROPE

Europe has about as much diversity, in terms of landscape, language, customs and culture, architecture and outlook, as most of us could absorb in a long and active lifetime. And most of it can be reached in less time than it takes to travel by train from London to Glasgow. There's just so much to see and to do, so many experiences to gather between the English Channel and the shores of the Black Sea. You could trace the route of the Danube by bike through ten extraordinary countries. You could become a pilgrim and walk in the steps of St Francis through Umbria to Rome, or follow the Robert Louis Stevenson Trail in the rolling hills of the Cévennes. There are adventures to be had on Corsica and Crete, wild country to explore in Andalucía and the Pyrenees, and enough all-season challenges among the stunning mountains of the Alps to satisfy the most rapacious of adrenalin junkies.

As we have found, adventures don't have to be of the scary kind, and even among the highest and most dramatic of mountain landscapes, there are countless days of true adventure and wonder to be had of a more pedestrian kind. These can be no less rewarding for being on a waymarked trail instead of a rock face.

◄ The last leg to Signal Forbes, with the needle-like Les Drus behind (photo: Kingsley Jones)

18 Signal Forbes

KINGSLEY JONES

Leaving the sleeping town of Chamonix-Mont-Blanc behind, I ran steeply upwards along forest trails. With each laboured breath escaping from my mouth, a small cloud immediately condensed in the crisp Alpine pre-dawn air; and with each gasp, my lungs were filled with the scent of larch. My shoes skimmed over the granite stones of the track. There was no noise apart from my breathing, the rhythmical scrunch of each step, and the rustle of my windproof jacket. It was a day off from guiding, and I was trail running up to Signal Forbes above the Mer de Glace, to watch sunrise over the glacier and the 4000m peaks of the Franco-Italian border.

In a few hours' time, these trails would be busy with hikers, climbers and runners, but for now they were just for me. No, not just me. A group of three young chamois suddenly darted across the path ahead, bounding off effortlessly into the forest. Alone again, I ran on upwards, revelling in the cool clean air filling my lungs, and the gentle burn of lactic acid in my leg muscles. Ahead, the trees opened out, and I ran over glacially polished slabs to arrive at the buvette at Les Mottets. I stopped to stare at the glacier below me, and my eyes moved upwards to take in the myriad of granite spires of the evocatively named Flammes de Pierre ridge of Les Drus.

The katabatic breeze soon cooled me, and I started to run upwards again, up the single-track trail to emerge below the Montenvers mountain railway station, then up the climbers' track to the imposing Victorian hotel. After a quick stop to refill my water bottle, I set off on what I consider to be the most magnificent kilometre of trail running in the Alps, ascending from Montenvers towards Signal Forbes. The trail zigzags in wide sweeps up the hillside, leaving the treeline far below, and I drank in the views ahead: the vast north face of the Grandes Jorasses, the Rochefort Arête, Dent du Géant and Aiguille du Charmoz. Below me, the steep hillside was covered with rhododendron and juniper, and below that was the bare ice of the glacier.

▲ Signal Forbes with its classic view of Les Drus

▷ Running the trail high above the Mer de Glace
(photos: Kingsley Jones)

'The most magnificent kilometre of trail running in the Alps'

Underfoot, the trail gave way from a dirt and gravel path to smooth granite blocks through a boulder field, eventually steepening in the final turns towards Signal Forbes. This viewpoint above the Mer de Glace is a small rocky plateau decorated with dozens of stone cairns, and beyond them rises the magnificent and impossibly vertical monolith of Les Drus. As I took in the view, the first shafts of sunlight burst through on either side of the summit. Despite the cool of dawn, I stood in the first beam of sunlight and raised my arms, feeling the warmth seeping into my body.

Standing there, in the light of the rising sun with the mountains to myself, I did not feel alone. I felt a deep connection to this environment, a sense of belonging, and at complete peace. It was time to move, and I ran onwards across the Grand Balcon Nord to Plan d'Aiguille, my feet eating up the kilometres. Off to the right, I could see the town of Chamonix, still nestled in the dawn gloom in the valley floor. Turning off the main track, I cut down through the Alpage de Blaitière, and into the forest once again. The larch needles cushioned each step, and I pushed fast, letting gravity help.

A coffee and croissant were waiting in my favourite café.

▲ Set among pine and larch trees, the cosy Burg Hut is accessible from Fiesch

19 The Aletschgletscher

KEV REYNOLDS

Perched on the lip of a glacier gorge on the eastern side of the Bernese Alps, the privately owned Burg Hut is one of my all-time favourites. I was there one summer with my daughter. I'd already spent three weeks on my own, finalising research for a guide to the Silvretta and Rätikon Alps, and still had a fortnight left to check a few routes for another book, so Claudia had decided the old man could do with some company.

We hiked up from Fiesch on one of those late-summer days when the last hay crop of the season was being taken. A field of autumn crocus opened to the sun and a cluster of larches gave the first hint of gold. We checked in at the hut and sat on the balcony knocking back cold drinks until dinner was served.

'Some places are just too good to keep to yourself'

She liked the Burg Hut as much as I did, and liked the view of the Fiescherhörner's snow-dusted walls even better when we set off next morning. That view filled our eyes as we climbed slabs behind the hut using fixed cable for support, but we lost it momentarily when weaving a course through a stand of birch, larch and fir, before emerging onto the crest of an old lateral moraine. And there, we not only regained the Fiescherhörner but caught sight of the distant reaches of the glacier that had carved out the gorge below.

A path angled round the valley's headwall, leading us up into a flat-bedded cleft between mountains where we were enticed into stopping for a bowl of soup at the Gletscherstube Märjela, another privately owned hut, overlooking the pools and shallow lakes

60

of the Märjelasee. Under clear skies, this is a magical region in which I've often wandered – sometimes alone, sometimes with my wife, and now with my daughter. You see, some places are just too good to keep to yourself. This is one of them.

Moments later we caught sight of the Aletschgletscher, the longest and by far the most impressive glacier in the Alps – a real highway of ice stretching for about 23km from the back of the Jungfrau to the Massa gorge below Riederfurka. That first view never fails to excite, and Claudia was soon leaping from one vantage point to the next with her camera, eager to record every sliced crevasse, every curving strip of moraine and every walling mountain.

For the rest of the afternoon, we wandered the trail that traces the course of the glacier down-valley, stopping frequently to look back, noting the great slabbed peaks shrinking with distance. Sometimes

we'd perch on a rock, legs dangling 50m above a yawning chasm of ice. I'd plan impossible routes on peaks opposite, content to know I'd never be put to the test, then we'd move on again, in no hurry to be anywhere but here.

At last, our trail climbed onto a ridge of juniper-carpeted moraine above the trees of the Aletschwald, to find the long line of the Pennine Alps suddenly revealed across the depths of the Rhône Valley. With Pennine Alps ahead, Bernese Alps behind, and Aletschgletscher below, I couldn't think of a better site for a bivouac.

But I was with my daughter, and I'd promised her a bed for the night, so we tripped along the ridge with the sun sinking fast, then plunged 400m down through larch woods to the Riederfurka Berghotel, from where we could look across the unseen Massa gorge to the lights of Belalp, our next destination. But Belalp could wait. This was perfection, and all we needed for now.

▼ Looking back on the Aletschgletscher from the ridge above the Aletschwald
(photo below and opposite: Kev Reynolds)

> 'The sun...painted the
> summit of Triglav a
> warm orange'

I felt fortunate because I was heading towards Bovški Gamsovec, one of my favourite peaks, for I knew that I would reap the rewards of peace and solitude, at least on the approach.

I'd arranged to meet three friends at a high pass – the Dovška vrata. They'd been staying overnight in the Pogačnikov dom on the other side. They would have breakfast, then meet me at the pass and we'd continue to the summit of Bovški Gamsovec together.

The early morning Alpine air added an extra zing to my step, so it wasn't long before I reached the junction where I parted from the Triglav 'highway'. Leaving the broad track, I headed up to the right on a narrower path, following signs for the Pogačnikov dom. Reaching the treeline, the view of Triglav's colossal north wall over my left shoulder confirmed what I'd come to believe – Bovški Gamsovec lets you appreciate Triglav in a deeper sense than actually climbing it does.

I was now on the steeply angled slope called the Sovatna, which leads to the pass. Turning my gaze from the stupendous views, I concentrated on the job at hand as the path led me up over bands of precipitous rock, clinging to the sides of gullies and grooves. As with any waymarked route in the Julian Alps, a well-placed metal peg or steel cable is always at hand here when needed.

As I gained height, I watched in awe as the sun first painted the summit of Triglav a warm orange, before its rays flooded the mountainside in front of me like liquid gold. Triglav's north wall began to reveal its myriad rock features as though a dark veil had been lifted.

I reached the pass with plenty of time in hand as I wasn't expecting my friends to join me for at least another hour. It was a beautiful morning but, as it was still only 7.30am, the air temperature had me digging in the rucksack for my fleece. No sooner had I put it on and sat down to

20 Bovški Gamsovec – a 'lesser' gem

ROY CLARK AND JUSTI CAREY

Most walkers and climbers who trek up the Vrata Valley on their first trip to the area will usually be heading for Triglav, the highest of the Julian Alps. This means, of course, that peaks of lesser height and fame are ignored or overlooked, regardless of their own unique character. I'd done it myself – I 'bagged' Triglav on my first Julian Alps trip, for whatever reason, be it understandable prioritising or egocentric illogical choice.

This time, though, I felt fortunate as I walked past the Aljažev dom (*dom* means 'mountain hut') in the Triglav National Park. No one was up yet; it was still dark in the forested valley, but as I looked up between the trees, I could detect a slight lightening of the sky – the first hint of dawn.

take in the view than a stone tumbled close by and I heard the sound of hooves clattering on the slabby rocks behind me. Standing up, I saw a large male ibex with huge ringed horns walking nonchalantly past, just metres away. Another five or six followed behind him. They were still close by when my friends joined me. Ibex photos taken, we left the pass for the final 45 minutes of ascent to the summit.

Gentians, edelweiss, bellflowers, laughter and smiles; a steep scramble that generated frowns and quiet concentration, then suddenly – we were on the summit.

It may seem that Bovški Gamsovec was created solely for the purpose of admiring its loftier neighbour, Triglav, but that would be an injustice to a smaller mountain of immeasurable qualities.

The balcony path high above the Engadine lakes

Pizzo Roseg dominates the path to Rifugio Marinelli Bombardieri
(photos: Gillian Price)

21 The Tour of the Bernina

GILLIAN PRICE

I'd been out of action for a while but finally got the go-ahead from the doctor to carry a rucksack again. Great news! So where to go that summer? Top of my list was a brand new route dipping in and out of Switzerland and Italy that I'd concocted to mark my return to Alpine trekking. The Tour of the Bernina ticked lots of boxes: it explores rugged landscapes well away from civilisation; strings together superbly located refuges and guesthouses; is a circuit so takes you back to where you began; is accessible to average walkers as it avoids glacier traverses; has a wealth of cultural and linguistic diversity; and, marvel of marvels, can be accessed by railway. All I had to do was go and walk it.

It was memorable even before we hit the trail, thanks to the train ride – not just any old train but the spectacular Bernina Express. After a thrilling ride over dizzy viaducts and up into the realm of giant mountains, the sleek red carriages deposited us at Passo del Bernina for the start of our adventure. It was mid August and we were blessed with brilliant weather, so no time was wasted. We just walked out of the railway station and onto the path. After a gentle ascent past tranquil tarns rimmed with flowers and over old moraines, all of a sudden we emerged on a dark rock ridge at the impressive 2973m Diavolezza lookout, finding ourselves high above a vast river of ice, the Pers Glacier – this was all that separated us from the Bernina and its snowy neighbours. From that very first day, I knew I was onto something special.

Two days on saw us heading up to cosy Chamanna Coaz, a unique hut all but hanging off the rock face below the Roseg Glacier. We spent an unforgettable night in that marvellous hut, thanks to the loudest snorer I have ever had the privilege to share a dormitory with...At one point during that never-ending night, four of us were yelling at him at the top of our voices – to no avail. Curiously, or not, he was the only cheery guest at the breakfast table...

Despite our sleep-deprived state that day, we were enchanted by the balcony route past the vast lakes of the Engadine. And I was especially chuffed to find my first ever purple gentian. A high rugged pass led south into Italy and a quiet pastoral world. We were made especially welcome at Rifugio Longoni by Elia with a delicious risotto, which we shared while the sun was setting on the light grey rock of Monte Disgrazia and its sprawling glacier. Another landmark stopover was at Lago Palù, where the hut manager was a huge fan of the Torino football team and insisted on giving us a T-shirt bearing their raging bull emblem.

The ensuing stage was pure magic – a drawn-out climb along the southern flanks of the Bernina group in the company of the magnificent crested pyramid of Pizzo Roseg. Moraine ridges and glacial-melt streams accompanied us to the amazing natural terrace occupied by Rifugio Marinelli Bombardieri, a haven in a sea of ice and snow and rock. It's just as well that photography is digital these days as I would have gone through rolls and rolls of film.

Back in Switzerland, nine days and 119km on, I drew up comparisons: Switzerland won on walnut tarts, trains and glaciers, while Italy dominated for rugged valleys, red wine and pizzoccheri pasta. The Tour of the Bernina is a winner on all fronts. I was not disappointed!

> 'From that very first day, I knew I was onto something special'

22 Sentiero de Luca and Via Ferrata delle Scalette

JAMES RUSHFORTH

Located in the Sesto Dolomites, the three monolithic towers that make up the world-famous Tre Cime di Lavaredo are undoubtedly one of my favourite places to climb, walk, ski and photograph. The stunning north faces are particularly impressive and it's easy to see why the middle tower, Cima Grande, is one of the prestigious six great north faces of the Alps. Perhaps the best vantage points from which to view these incredible features are the nearby peaks of Monte Paterno and Torre Toblino. While researching a climbing guidebook with long-term climbing partner Lynne Hempton, I was able to visit both of these superbly situated summits on the same day, combining Sentiero de Luca/Innerkofler and Via Ferrata delle Scalette to create a magical circuit.

We begin with the logical approach from Rifugio Auronzo, the considerable length of our chosen route necessitating an early start. Despite the cold clear air, a thin mist settles above the lake at Auronzo, diffracting the dawn light and creating several tiny rainbows that hang precariously above the valley. We quickly reach Rifugio Lavaredo and turn north to ascend more steeply towards Forcella Lavaredo and the bluff buttress that marks the base of Monte Paterno. A further short traverse on the west side of the ridge brings us to the first of several characteristic tunnels that date back to World War I. As we proceed through the dark and claustrophobic setting, I idly wonder about the route's namesakes, local mountain guides Piero de Luca and Sepp Innerkofler, who served here during the 'white war', a conflict that would see Innerkofler fall to his death defending this very peak. Soon, however, as the tunnel angles upwards and we abruptly exit into the welcoming rays of the July sunshine, such thoughts are banished as we take in the warm glow and the glorious view before us. The route continues to weave along the ridge with easy but enjoyable climbing to reach the conical summit of Monte Paterno.

After taking a few moments to admire the spectacular panorama, we press on, descending through a further system of tunnels and impressive rock towers to reach the beautifully situated Rifugio Locatelli. Although the sun has only just passed its zenith, there are already several fellow hikers enjoying a beer and it takes more than a little willpower to resist the urge to join them. With a twinge of regret, we continue northwards, passing behind the rocky outcrop of Sasso di Sesto to reach the base of Torre Toblino and the start of Via Ferrata delle Scalette. This route is immediately steeper, offering technical climbing as the wire feeds directly up the first headwall to reach the first of the many metal ladders that give the route its name. A final easier scramble leads to the summit and one of the best views in the Dolomites, where we take the opportunity to appreciate some rare solitude as we admire the scene. The descent down the east side of the peak requires concentration, with some interesting down-climbing to rejoin the path to Rifugio Locatelli.

With the summer solstice having occurred just a few days earlier, the sun sets on the north faces of the Tre Cime, illuminating the vast walls in golden light. Night falls and the stars quite literally align, the Milky Way hanging just above the towers as we finally indulge in the aforementioned beer. Our good intentions to walk back and complete the circuit wane in the moonlight and after a kind offer of some local grappa and a bed for the night, we gladly accept!

'the sun sets on...the Tre Cime, illuminating the vast walls in golden light'

23 Stubai honeymoon

ALLAN HARTLEY

We married in late October 1967. With no money for a honeymoon, we chose to save for a holiday the next year. A friend recommended we join the Austrian Alpine Club and make a hut-to-hut tour, suggesting the Stubai Alps near Innsbruck as being really good.

Duly enthused, we joined in January 1968. The membership cards arrived, together with a brochure advertising holidays and tours organised by FW Inghams of Bond Street in London. Most tours were way beyond our means, but we guessed we could afford Independent Touring at £14 each and follow the programme for the Stubai Rucksack Route, so in July we set off on our would-be honeymoon for what would be the first of many hut-to-hut tours.

From home in Radcliffe, we travelled to Manchester for the overnight bus to London, transferring in the morning for the London Victoria to Dover train, then ferry to Ostend. At Ostend we were met by

the sleeper coach (nicknamed 'the travelling hut', a specially designed coach with seats that could be converted into bunks), and left in the early afternoon heading for Germany. At a service station, everyone got off so the seats could be converted into bunks, then setting off again we drove through the night, stopping in the morning at Kufstein on the German–Austrian border for passport checks. Here, the bunks became seats again. Our next stop was Wörgl for those going to the Venediger, then Jenbach for those booked on Zillertal Rock and Ice Training courses. We were at Innsbruck railway station just after 10am and on our own at last.

I couldn't find the bus stop for Neustift in the Stubaital, but a bogus taxi guy spotted us looking lost and asked where we were going. When I said Neder near Neustift, he said fine and told us how much; then, fearing we might be abducted, we set off. Contrary to our fears, he dropped us where we asked, which gave us a five-hour walk up the Pinnistal valley, surrounded by mountains, to reach our first night's lodging at the Innsbrucker Hut. How brilliant – all anxious thoughts evaporated! But the next problem on our steep learning curve was what to eat, for neither of us spoke German other than 'please', 'thank you' and 'beer'.

Scanning what other folk were having, we settled for what would be our staple for several days: soup and bread, with a shared cake. Our travel package included vouchers as payment for *Übernachtung* (overnight accommodation): one voucher for the *Matratzenlager* (literally 'mattress room') and two for a bed. Needless to say, being skint, we had the *Matratzenlager* in the roof.

Next day we bagged our first Alpine peak, the Habicht, being chastised on the way up by those on the way down: '*Engländer*, you start too late!' But we progressed and learned as we made our way on what is now known as the Stubaier Höhenweg. I managed to blag my way into joining a couple of groups to climb the Wilder Freiger and Schaufelspitze; the days passed too quickly and soon the tour was over.

Back in Innsbruck, we waited for the coach to take us home. It didn't arrive. The drivers had their dates mixed up. One had to be dragged out of bed after just finishing a shift; the other was a 'no-show' – which meant we had one driver to make the long journey to Ostend with passengers talking to him throughout the night to keep him awake.

But who would have thought that, 50 years after standing on the Schaufelspitze, I would become president of the Austrian Alpine Club (UK)?

< The author's wife on a honeymoon
ascent of the Trögler

> Allan Hartley on the Schaufelspitze in 1968
(photos: Allan Hartley)

24 Circling the Silvretta

KEV REYNOLDS

The summit of Piz Linard, highest of the Silvretta Alps, has always eluded me. A rope's length from the top, I managed to dislodge a rock onto my wife's head. She wasn't wearing a helmet at the time, and although the wound was not life-threatening, it was bad enough to hasten a retreat to administer first aid.

We'd only been married a few months.

Four decades later, we gazed on our old nemesis from the Vereina Pass, from where the mountain appeared much more benign than it had from the south all those years ago. But we had no desire to give it another crack, for now we were making a tour of the Silvretta Alps, and Piz Linard was merely acting as a cornerstone.

Six of us had begun by taking a minibus taxi from Klosters to Berghaus Vereina, a charming inn-like hut in a peaceful location, and after spending a night there set out for the first pass of our planned circuit. It was early summer and we had the world to ourselves. We also had a torrent of snowmelt to wade through, thanks to a missing footbridge. It took an hour before our feet began to thaw out.

The following day took us through the exquisite village of Guarda and up into Val Tuoi, among meadows so thick with flowers there was no room for grass to grow, and we spent the night at the foot of Piz Buin in the newly refurbished Tuoi Hut.

Piz Buin was turned upside down in a semi-frozen lake on the way to the rocky saddle of the Furcletta on a two-pass day, but we lost it on our descent into Val d'Urezzas and wouldn't see it again for another couple of days. Crossing Pass Futschöl later that afternoon, we traded Swiss sunshine for Austrian rain and made good use of the drying facilities at the Jamtal Hut. It was still raining when we trekked to the Wiesbadener Hut, so the glaciated north flank of Piz Buin was hidden from view until breakfast on our sixth day. But clouds descended once more as we made a crossing of the Litzner Sattel en route to the Saarbrücker Hut, so the mountains contained their mystery until – glory be! – on the morning of our seventh day I stepped outside the hut to be greeted by early sunlight flooding peaks and ridges we'd crossed in ignorance only yesterday.

The world had been transformed.

> 'Piz Buin was turned upside down in a semi-frozen lake'

So too had the glacier I'd crossed seven years earlier on the far side of the Kromerlücke above the hut. Then, it had stretched virtually from the pass to the spine of the Mittelrücke; now it had shrunk so much that to reach ice involved a heart-in-mouth descent of almost vertical snow-covered scree. We were all heartily relieved to reach the Mittelrücke after that, and slogged our way up to the frontier ridge where, at last, we could relax to enjoy a wondrous panorama of ragged peaks, snowfields and dying glaciers. (When I returned the following year to finalise research for the guidebook, I found an alternative route to avoid the horror of the Kromerlücke descent.)

A vague path teetering along the frontier ridge brought us to our final pass of the circuit. From the Plattenjoch we could look down on the Tübinger Hut on the Austrian flank, into the deep Seetal on the Swiss side, and across to the Gross and Klein Seehorn peaks that would guard our long descent into Val Sardasca, the pastoral valley draining down to Klosters, which would effectively close our tour of the Silvretta Alps.

> 'Take time to enjoy this belvedere – the views are among the finest in the Alps'

25 The Zermatt Safari

BILL O'CONNOR

I have a passion for ski touring and love the fact that you have to 'earn your turns'. That said, there are powder days, snatched between spells of poor weather, when you can earn your turns by paying for them. Zermatt is a skiers' hub, an overgrown village at the foot of the world's most recognisable peak, and the beginning and end of so many great skiing adventures. But don't overlook its potential as a ski-safari paradise. By using its lift system, you can get the most 'pow' for your £ on a blue-sky day.

Push ennui aside and go for an early lift. Take the Sunnegga underground lift that links with the cable car to Unterrothorn (3013m) and let the skiing begin! Turn north into the Tufterchumme and descend 1100m in open and then wooded terrain between pistes to the Patrullarve lift, which will carry you back to the Unterrothorn.

The next stage is a descent by piste to Fluhalp, followed by plenty of off-piste action on the south-facing slopes of the Roter Bodmen. Strong-willed safari aficionados whizz past Fluhalp, while wiser whizzers will stop for coffee and *tarte aux myrtilles* (blueberry tart) – after all, there's a long way to go. Refreshed and sustained, continue descending to Gant, with plenty of opportunity for fresh tracks either side of the piste.

Catch your breath while waiting for the lift to the Hohtälli (3286m) and then take the link to the Rote Nase. Those scouting for off-piste potential will have seen the vast slope under the lift, which offers stunning skiing after a fresh fall of snow. Early risers will have time to fit in its descent and return to the cable car. From the Rote Nase, you can descend the slopes alongside the Triftji piste and use drag lifts to gain Pt.3405m, which in the past was the end of the old Stockhorn lift. Now boot eastwards along the ridge for about 1km to the Stockhorn (3532m) itself – it's well worth the effort. From the Stockhorn, turn north along a broad ridge towards Pt.3356m. Take the open, north-west-facing slopes of the Triftjigletscher, descending a full 1300m back to Gant. After a fresh fall of snow, this descent is as good as it gets.

Having returned to Hohtälli, descend the piste to Breitboden. There's plenty of untracked terrain either side of the piste, but avoid dropping to Grünsee. Continue descending via Riffelalp to Furi at 1864m.

The next stage of the safari is truly spectacular. Various lifts follow to Trockener Steg and then Furggsattel (3351m). Take time to enjoy

△ Sallie O'Connor and Ben Holt boot along the ridge from the Rote Nase to the Stockhorn

^ Ben Holt and Sallie O'Connor descend the Unterer Theodulgletscher below the Matterhorn
(photos: Bill O'Connor)

this belvedere – the views are among the finest in the Alps. Once off the chairlift, descend 100m or so to traverse under Pt.3384m. Traverse the open slopes of the Oberer Theodulgletscher north-west towards Pt.3181m. Bear west to traverse south of a rock island and continue descending the delightful slopes of the Furggletscher under the east face of the Matterhorn before joining a piste at Hirli to Furgg (2432m) – spectacular. For the leg-weary, it's possible to descend by lift or on piste to Zermatt.

You are now on the last leg of your safari. Take the lift to Schwarzsee and then the piste to Stafelalp as it arcs below the north face of the Matterhorn, offering glorious views of Dent Blanche, Obergabelhorn and other 4000ers. For lovers of tree skiing, given the right conditions it's possible to turn northwards off the track and descend steeply through wooded slopes to join the piste to Furi. From there, the piste descends directly to Zermatt at the end of a spectacular day's skiing, giving close to 7000m of descent.

26 Valscura

JAMES RUSHFORTH

Carving a striking, perpendicular and impossibly steep line down the south-east face of Sassongher, the Valscura Couloir is undoubtedly one of the great ski-mountaineering descents of the Dolomites. The itinerary enjoys a foreboding reputation due to the notorious rarity of finding favourable conditions: the south-easterly aspect of the descent encourages ice and hard, 'cruddy' snow, while the approach that traverses through the cliffs above Colfosco can be particularly dangerous with a poorly bonded and untransformed snowpack.

Having regularly observed the gully from the sun-lit pistes of Pralongia, I was determined to make a free-ride descent in good powder snow, a challenge that would require a great deal of patience and some careful timing. The opportunity finally arose during a particularly spectacular season after several days of steady snow and unusually light winds.

> 'What followed was some of the best couloir skiing I've done'

Forecasts were predicting a cloudy day with attenuating snow; if accurate, this would prevent the traverse from getting dangerously warm and protect the snow from the sun. Setting out with fellow skier Katie Keeley, we opted for an early start to ensure the temperatures stayed suitably low throughout the approach. Unfortunately, our 5am departure meant that the ski lifts which would have saved us 400m of ascent were not yet running, but the icy corduroy made for quick progress as we skinned up the side of the piste to leave the ski resort paraphernalia behind. As we struck out north-east, making numerous kick-turns towards the start of the traverse, the sun rose and transformed the darkness to grey mist, the forecasted low cloud settling just above our heads.

As the surrounding landscape narrowed and became more exposed, we swapped our skis and poles for crampons and

◁ Descending the upper half of the
Valscura Couloir in deep snow

△ The Valscura Couloir cuts down the east (right) side of
the Sassongher, the main peak of the range
(photos: James Rushforth)

mountaineering axes. Progress slowed as the terrain became increasingly technical, the reduced surface area of the crampons causing us to sink through the fresh snow with each step. With visibility down to around 5 metres, I broke trail using the looming rock walls above as a point of reference.

After several hours, the ledge system widened enough to allow us to switch back to skins and we soon made faster headway towards the saddle of Forcella Sassongher, our skis planing on top of the deep snow. Aided with ski crampons, the final 100 metres were overcome with some steep kick-turns which brought us to just below the summit of Sassongher and the start of the couloir. Although the swirling cloud prevented a clear view down the vertiginous chute, there was just enough visibility to glimpse the perfect aesthetics of the upper couloir before it disappeared back into the mist.

The usual preparations ensued – transceiver check, boots buckled down, skins off, bindings clear of snow, harness on – a soothing and familiar ritual. With a final check to ensure the snowpack was stable, we dropped in and began the much-anticipated descent. What followed was some of the best couloir skiing I've done, the flexing of the ski and subsequent rebound of the snow creating that wonderful sensation of flying that one has to experience to truly understand. Alas, the descent was over all too quickly as 1000m of hard-fought height gain quickly condensed into a series of short but wonderfully satisfying turns. With a final 15m abseil to overcome a blind rocky drop, we returned to the valley, the enduring exhilaration of the moments before more than compensating for the somewhat less than elegant swim through the thick dwarf pines to reach the main road.

Of the many wonderful experiences in the Dolomites, there are some that give truth to the old adage: good things come to those who wait.

▲ Walking through fields of grain in the
Gattaceca Reserve, just 30km from
Rome (photo: Jacqueline Zeindlinger)

27 The Way of St Francis

SANDY BROWN

'Maybe St James won't mind if we change our allegiance to St Francis,' wrote my Austrian pilgrim friend, Jacqueline, in early 2013. 'I found some info on the internet about this trail in Italy that follows the life of St Francis of Assisi. Let's do it for our annual hike!'

A few months later, armed with an Italian phrase book, my college Spanish and Jacqueline's enthusiasm, we two former Camino de Santiago pilgrims and a couple of other friends trekked the olive groves, forests and fields of beautiful Umbria and Lazio, walking from picturesque Assisi to majestic Rome. The more we walked, the more we fell in love with St Francis and his amazing homeland.

Jonathan Williams at Cicerone took little convincing about the worthiness of a Way of St Francis book, so the following year I said goodbye to my job and headed to Central Italy.

After four fun weeks of Italian studies with college students in Perugia, I boarded the train to Florence and began a long, solitary climb into the gloomy and glorious Casentino National Forest. Soon I was lucky to stumble upon an energetic group of female German pilgrims, who welcomed me into their group. In the evenings we shared a bottle or two of Umbria's Sagrantino wine and told stories of our pilgrim adventures. We enjoyed the steep climbs together, always keeping a sharp lookout for the wild boar that make this region home. As luck would have it, we arrived at the lofty and serene mountaintop convent

▲ The Coronation of the Virgin fresco by Fra Filippo in the Spoleto Duomo apse (photo: Sandy Brown)

of Santuario della Verna the night of a pipe organ concert there. The next day, strolling among the colourful frescoes of St Francis, the pilgrims and I said our goodbyes, before they headed back home to work and family.

My faithful friend, Jacqueline, met me the next day and we caught up on old times as we trekked downward into the Upper Tiber River Valley. We found medieval towns like Città di Castello and Gubbio to be like precious gems in a glimmering, antique necklace. We made our way through the sunflower-dappled countryside just north of Assisi and then, exhausted and exhilarated after many days of walking, climbed the final hill into the radiant, pink-stoned hometown of St Francis.

Although Jacqueline had to return home, my wife, Theresa, joined me. Like honeymooners, we snapped selfies in front of the mighty Marmore waterfall, built by the Romans and still the tallest human-made waterfall in the world. After five days of olive groves, a few wild boars, and delicious food in hospitable Sabine villages, we arrived at

> 'Olive groves, a few wild boars, and delicious food in hospitable Sabine villages'

our final destination – the statues, museums and churches of Vatican City. I stayed below, in the safe confines of St Peter's Basilica, while Theresa took pictures from the lofty cupola.

Back in Perugia, I began the work of collecting my notes and GPS tracks and writing the book's walking descriptions. Here, I was fortunate to meet leaders of Sviluppumbria, Umbria's economic development agency, who agreed to sponsor a launch party at the 2015 World Travel Market in London. The little book project seemed a smart investment for tourism-inclined Umbria, and it hasn't disappointed.

Today, when I walk these trails in Central Italy, I see pilgrims from around the world with little blue Cicerone guidebooks in their hands, and wonder what adventurous spirit brought them here, if their legs are hurting, if they've seen a boar, and whether, like me, they find the flavour of beautiful Umbria in an evening glass of Sagrantino.

Alès and to write an account of his adventures. His only companion was a heavily laden donkey, which he christened Modestine. Twelve days later, he walked into the small town of Saint-Jean-du-Gard, west of Alès. Footsore, frustrated with the antics of Modestine and eager for news of Fanny, but with enough copy in his journal to write his planned book, he sold the donkey and took a coach to Alès. He later left for America, married Fanny, wrote *Treasure Island* and became a celebrated author. But it all started with his Cévennes adventure.

A little over 100 years later, in 1987, I too set out from Le Monastier, armed with a copy of Stevenson's original journal and a French leaflet with brief details of a possible path. A route had earlier been poorly waymarked but was difficult to follow and the French authorities at the time were not interested in a hike taken by a foreign author a century before. I met no other walkers and the locals were baffled as to what I was doing. With perseverance, I worked out a good route, which was first published by Cicerone in 1992. Not long afterwards, the French changed their opinion and created an official trail, the GR70. Today, thousands walk the Chemin de Stevenson each year, France's second most popular long-distance walk. Everyone in the region is now aware of RLS and his sojourn all those years ago, and many are making their livelihood out of the trail.

The RLS Trail is a scenic delight, meandering south from Le Monastier through delightful rural countryside, passing a number of picturesque small towns, villages and hamlets, crossing the high plateau of Mont Lozère and continuing through the wooded hills of the Cévennes, before journey's end at Saint-Jean.

RLS has become a part of my life: I've followed his travels around the globe, in California and the South Pacific, even visiting his grave high on a hill in Samoa, where he settled for the last years of his short life. You don't have to go that far, but do consider the RLS Trail for your next walking holiday, as this superb route is sure to delight. Take not only the Cicerone guidebook, but also a copy of *Travels with a Donkey*, so you can compare RLS's adventures with your own. A lot has changed since 1878, but many features are exactly as he described: ancient roadside crosses, traditional buildings, a historic monastery hidden deep in woodland, and of course the 'indescribable air of the South', as RLS put it. When walking this trail, there's a feeling that one is 'walking with ghosts', as all the characters Stevenson described, children and all, are long since gone; you gain an understanding of your own mortality. The RLS Trail has it all.

28 The Robert Louis Stevenson Trail

ALAN CASTLE

France, with its variety of landscapes and extensive network of Grande Randonnée (GR) routes, offers some of the best trail walking in Europe. Apart from hiking, another of my passions is literature, and from an early age the Scottish writer Robert Louis Stevenson has been one of my favourite authors. So it was hardly surprising that the route taken by RLS described in his first successful book, *Travels with a Donkey in the Cévennes*, published in 1879 and still in print today, would fascinate me.

In the autumn of 1878, a young Stevenson, madly in love with the American Fanny Osbourne and desperate to write a successful book that would launch his writing career, set out on foot from the small village of Le Monastier-sur-Gazeille, near Le Puy-en-Velay. His aim was to cross the Velay and Cévennes in south-eastern France to the town of

⌃ The old path that descends into Goudet

⌂ Woodcarving of Robert Louis Stevenson and Modestine in Le Bouchet-Saint-Nicolas
(photos: Alan Castle)

29 From ocean to sea through the Pyrenees

BRIAN JOHNSON

As a young man, I followed a common pattern among British walkers; I discovered the delights of Wales, the Lake District and Scotland, and completed the Pennine Way as my first backpacking trip. Time to venture abroad, I explored the Alps and the Dolomites and managed ascents of some of the easier big peaks, including Mont Blanc. Then I picked up the French guide by Georges Véron to the Haute Randonnée Pyrénéenne (HRP) and, over four years, walked from the Atlantic Ocean to the Mediterranean Sea; I have now walked from Ocean to Sea more than ten times along the HRP, GR11 and GR10, and have not been back to the Alps since!

Why have I fallen in love with the Pyrenees rather than the Alps? The principle charm of these mountains is the wilderness experience which is still on offer. When I first visited them 35 years ago, you could find solitude almost anywhere. Now there are tourist hot spots such as Gavarnie, Ordesa and Andorra, but much of the range is relatively quiet and you can still find remote corners, seemingly untouched by man.

The Pyrenees are every bit as good as the Alps when it comes to scenery; the predominant limestone and granite rock types, together with extensive glaciation in the ice ages, have resulted in jagged peaks, impressive snowfields, deep canyons, high passes, big rock walls, alpine meadows, dramatic waterfalls, cascading streams, lakes and sparkling tarns.

Renowned for their wildflower meadows, along with the butterflies they support, the Pyrenees are also a Mecca for birdwatchers, who will particularly appreciate the birds of prey – including the massive griffon vulture, which you will see most days. You can also expect to see Egyptian vulture, red kite, black kite, buzzard, honey buzzard, kestrel, sparrowhawk, goshawk and peregrine falcon, as well as golden, booted, short-toed and Bonelli's eagles and possibly the rare lammergeier or even a migrating osprey. You will have frequent sightings of chamois and marmot.

The Pyrenees are much less commercialised than the Alps, with fewer people, cars, ski resorts and regulations but more unspoilt villages, more charm and a greater sense of freedom. The wild camping is second to none. I value the relative quiet and the opportunities for skinny-dipping in mountain tarns and streams under the hot sun.

The range is extremely varied, with the green rolling hills of the Basque Country giving way to spectacular alpine mountains of the High Pyrenees, and more arid mountains as you approach the Mediterranean. It is a land of many cultures; the Basque Country and Catalonia were once proud independent nations and still have their own languages and customs, while in the Central Pyrenees, it is French or Spanish culture that is predominant. With the prevailing wind blowing from the north-west, the Basque Country and north-facing valleys of France get more than their fair share of mist and rain, but south of the watershed, and in the east, you can expect mostly warm sunny days.

'The attraction of wild camping in the spectacular valleys and on remote mountain ridges'

Exploring a chain about 400km long whose hills rise steeply from the Atlantic and drop steeply to the Mediterranean, the three main coast-to-coast routes (GR10, GR11 and HRP) provide an 800–900km traverse on well-marked trails through France, Spain and Andorra. While it is possible to walk from coast to coast using hotels, hostels and mountain refuges, it is the attraction of wild camping in the spectacular valleys and on remote mountain ridges that has led to my returning time after time to the Pyrenees.

It is the freedom of the wilderness!

> A solitary overnight camp below the Sierra d'Alano while trekking the GR11 (photo: Brian Johnson)

◄ The summit of La Torrecilla rewards with an immense panoramic view

▶ The old Roman drinking troughs of El Pilar de Tolox

(photos: Guy Hunter-Watts)

30 Climbing La Torrecilla

GUY HUNTER-WATTS

West of Ronda in southern Spain, the villages of the Grazalema Natural Park are linked by a network of drovers' paths which wind through groves of olive and almond and ancient stands of holm and gall oaks. To the south, a vast forest of cork oak stretches nearly all the way to Gibraltar, while out east a high massif rises majestically above the town. This is the Sierra de las Nieves, a UNESCO Biosphere Reserve, which is often (as its name suggests) blanketed in snow during the winter months.

The park's most challenging trail, and one close to my heart, leads to the summit of La Torrecilla (1919m), the massif's highest peak. From the summit, you're treated to one of the most bone-thrilling vistas to be found in Andalucía. The 360-degree panorama encompasses the Sierra Nevada, a long stretch of the Mediterranean coast, Málaga, Gibraltar and the Strait, while on clear days the Rif mountains of northern Morocco rise hazily above a glittering sea.

'One of the wildest tracts of mountain terrain in southern Spain'

The adventure begins with a drive along 10km of rutted track leading to the trailhead and the mountain refuge of Los Quejigales. Crossing a narrow bridge that spans a babbling stream – it can become a torrent in the winter months – your first challenge comes in the form of a rocky path which zigzags steeply up through the largest stand of Spanish firs or pinsapos in the Sierra. These Ice Age relics are the botanical jewel of the park, a species found only in Andalucía, the Moroccan Rif and remote parts of the Caucasus. The forest is a sculptural wonderland of twisted trunks, some up to 30m in height. It's even more beautiful when the ancient trees are cloaked in the mist that often licks round the mountain early in the day.

Breaking out of the forest, you reach a high, windy ridge as the Med comes into view. Here, the trail loops north then back south before adopting a course towards La Torrecilla. Passing an ancient ice pit, the path runs through a swathe of gall oaks. The forest suffered greatly at a time when its wood supplied the shipyards of the Atlantic coast: the tiny caravel that carried Columbus west to America was almost certainly built of oak from the Ronda mountains. Further devastation came at the hands of charcoal burners who worked the forest until just 50 years back. The trees are now a protected species and thriving once again, aided by restrictions placed on the grazing of goats.

The waymarked trail runs on past the entrance to the pothole Sima GESM. Explored to 1100m, this is one of the deepest potholes in Europe and was discovered just 40 years ago. Here, the path crosses a series of flat-bottomed dolines, or depressions in the limestone, their baize-like grass strangely reminiscent of neatly tended golfing greens. Cutting through a cleft in the rocks, you come to the spring and Roman drinking troughs of El Pilar de Tolox. This is the place to replenish your water bottle before tackling the final 200m of ascent to the summit, now high above the treeline.

After gulping in the dizzy views from this extraordinary natural mirador, you need to retrace your footsteps back down to the ice pit passed early in the walk. From here, a second path loops further north, leading down through a second stand of magnificent pinsapos, to bring you back to the trailhead after some six hours of exhilarating trail. Not only is this hike fascinating from a botanical and historical perspective, but it also takes you to the heart of one of the wildest tracts of mountain terrain in southern Spain – a 'must-walk' should you come to explore the trails close to Ronda.

31 Cycling through history on the Danube Cycleway

MIKE WELLS

We stood on the newest part of Europe: not a country just admitted to the EU, but a bare sandbank on the edge of the Black Sea, so recently formed that it appears on no maps. There was no vegetation, but this will soon arrive as neighbouring islands that have formed over recent decades already sprout stubby bushes. This is part of the Danube Delta, a vast area of wetland where the River Danube reaches the sea and deposits sediment to form new land.

We had reached the sandbank by small boat from the Romanian coastal resort village of Sulina. This was the final point on a trip that had started nearly 3000km away in a shaded woodland clearing near Martinskapelle, high in southern Germany's Black Forest. Here, a small trickle of water bubbles up beneath a few rocks and a plaque describes a river that flows for 2888km, passing through eight countries, more than any other river on earth. Although only erected in the 1960s, this plaque is already out of date, the break-ups of Yugoslavia and the Soviet Union having increased the number of countries to ten.

From Black Forest spring to Black Sea sandbank we cycled downhill for five weeks on the Danube Cycleway, using mostly quiet roads, good cycle tracks and flood dykes that follow the river on what

'From Black Forest spring to Black Sea sandbank we cycled downhill for five weeks'

is probably the most varied long-distance cycle ride in Europe. Eight different languages are spoken, with the river known by seven different names. Waymarking varied from near-perfect in Austria and Serbia through inconsistent but improving in Hungary to non-existent in Romania.

It was a journey through the geography of a continent. On the way, we passed through seven great gorges, starting with the narrow winding Donautal through the Schwäbische Alb and ending with the Iron Gates gorges where the river has forced a gap between Carpathian and Balkan mountain chains. Between these gorges we cycled through pretty valleys and extensive plains, including the Great Hungarian Plain, which took three days to cross, and the even larger Wallachian Plain in southern Romania, which needed five. These features offer a kaleidoscope of colour, with great white limestone cliffs and green forests in the gorges, red paprika crops in Hungary and yellow sunflowers in Wallachia – and, according to Johann Strauss, the blue of the river itself, although this is probably a bit of wishful thinking as we found the river to be mostly a silvery grey.

Then there are the myriad towns and cities that represent 2000 years of European history. En route we climbed the spire of Ulm's medieval cathedral, the tallest religious building in the world. We visited the great baroque abbeys of Melk and Klosterneuburg, built by the Habsburgs to demonstrate their support of the Catholic Church. We crossed the former Iron Curtain from Austria into Slovakia using what is nowadays a permanently open blue gate. We climbed to the ramparts of Visegrád castle, first residence of the kings of Hungary. We visited Zemun, where Austrian artillery fired the initial shots of World War I across the river into Belgrade, and in Drobeta-Turnu Severin we saw the remaining fragments of the great bridge that Roman Emperor Trajan had built across the Danube in order to invade Dacia (present day Romania).

And of course there were the two great imperial cities of Vienna and Budapest, with their grand thoroughfares, royal palaces, imposing cathedrals, national parliaments, important museums, leading art galleries, opera houses and concert halls. Our route followed riverside cycle tracks through the centres of both cities. The ride would have been worth doing if only to visit them; everything else was a bonus!

Riverside cycle tracks take the Danube Cycleway through Budapest
(photos: Mike Wells)

32 The White Mountains of Crete

LORAINE WILSON

Decades ago, I led a commercial group on an exploratory trip in the White Mountains. I had led treks here before, climbing several accessible peaks and following traditional mule tracks over the range, but on this occasion I wanted to explore a route shown dotted on the small-scale maps of the time – a traverse of the central massif from west to east on what I supposed to be a mule track of sorts.

From the highest summit, we surveyed the tops in conjunction with map and compass and planned our initial stage, which, it appeared, would cut off one-third of the 'dotted' route. As the weather was ideal, we returned down to our campsite, filled four spare 5-litre water bottles, and set off to the first pass, which would provide us with a closer view.

By now we were used to the high desert scenery, but even that did not prepare us for the view we were to see on reaching the pass. We found ourselves gazing across an extraordinary and somewhat menacing landscape of greys and blacks; of jagged rocks and ridges, scree, lumps and formations, huge pits and, beyond, great conical peaks faced with massive stone slabs pitted with cracks.

Well, our next move, as far as I was concerned, was to join the route of the path, because that is as much a safety feature on these mountains as any other. But when we did actually get there after making our way through the maze, I was dismayed to find no trace of footpath at all! Looking all around, we might never have guessed we were in Crete, or

Trekkers on an old mule track in the White Mountains

The high desert crossed without the aid of footpaths
(photos: Loraine Wilson)

Europe, or anywhere else any of us had ever seen. And we knew this would not be an easy walk to do alone. Astonished by the unfolding scene, we pressed on as best we could and, as evening arrived, reached the destination we had noted from far away that morning.

With the moonscape now behind us, we planned another hour's walking. There was a little greenery here, and I thought shepherds' paths would soon make the going easier, but this was not to be. Still far from human contact, we struggled across a vast scree slope spewing from the long mountain above. Far below, we spotted the treeline and worked our way down to it, where a few cypress trees made for a relatively cosy bivouac. Dinner over, we went to bed on our water ration, thinking obsessively of liquid in all its forms.

A cup of tea all round next morning, another careful sharing out of our water ration and we set off, although we had to gain height once

> 'Looking all around, we might never have guessed we were in Crete, or Europe'

more. I was following a slightly lower route when, after just an hour's effort, I heard shouts from those above: a sheep trough had been seen down below. We'd made it! I had the pleasure of raising the first bucket, watching the water shimmer as it came up. What a tea party we had!

Refreshed, we continued our descent through upland valleys rich in trees and shrubs, and then steeply down on a mule track to Ammoudari, a village on the Askifou plain. I knew the proprietor of the *kafeneon* (café) and wanted to celebrate; but alas, a funeral had cast a gloom over everyone there. Subdued, we decided to catch a bus down to the coast; but just before we climbed aboard, the café owner whispered: 'Lefka Ori?' ('White Mountains?')

'Yes,' was my hushed reply, 'it looked like the moon up there!'

87

33 The GR20

PADDY DILLON

The GR20 through the mountains of Corsica has a reputation that precedes it. They say it's the toughest waymarked trail in Europe, and I can't disagree with that as I've never found anything tougher. Not with waymarks, anyway. You can always find a tough route just by stepping off the beaten track. The thing about the GR20 is that the beaten track itself is often alarmingly steep, rocky and exposed.

I once met Alan and Beryl Castle, who trekked the GR20 while preparing Cicerone's original guide to the route. They said it was terrifying and they'd never go back. In fact, the only other people I knew who'd embarked on the trek had given up after the first day. When I was offered the chance to write a new guidebook, it was because another writer, Constance Roos, had died after being struck by lightning while researching the route.

> 'Trekkers rooted to the spot, crying tears of fear, while angrily swearing in many languages'

To be honest, I was more than a little apprehensive about accepting this project.

Apprehension gave way to bouts of stomach-churning fear, almost on a daily basis, as I would find myself in situations I normally try to avoid. I'm not happy on steep rock and the GR20 had an abundance of it. Of course, in those days the route went through the notorious Cirque de la Solitude, where I witnessed trekkers rooted to the spot, crying tears of fear, while angrily swearing in many languages.

To cut short what seemed like a recurring nightmare, the trek was completed, all variants and alternatives checked and a new guidebook was published.

The thing about a popular route and a popular guidebook is that things change over time and the best way to deal with changes is to go and check everything again. So, I found myself back in Corsica, back on the GR20.

While the route was fundamentally the same, it seemed somehow different. I'd been before and I had my own guidebook with me. I quite literally knew what was round every corner, and it made all the difference. The fear and apprehension were gone – even in the Cirque de la Solitude – and I was able to enjoy the scale and majesty of the mountains, providing I watched where I was putting my hands and feet. Heck – I even doubled back and went through the Cirque again!

Every so often, someone would look at me, mutter something to their companion, flick through the pages of my guidebook and ask, 'Are you Paddy Dillon?' An Icelandic woman on the trail went one better: 'Excuse me, do I know you?' she asked.

'Well, you might be using my guidebook,' I replied.

'So I am,' she said, after checking, then added, 'You came into my tourist office in Iceland, asking about the Lónsöræfi Trail.'

Another Cicerone author, Hilary Sharp, was in Corsica when a disaster unfolded on the GR20 in 2015, and she passed on the news. Despite a bad weather forecast and advice against heading into the mountains, dozens of trekkers embarked on the traverse of the Cirque de la Solitude. There was a landslide. Seven were killed instantly and many more were injured. The Cirque was closed the following day and never reopened.

Sitting in the comfort of my armchair, trying to keep on top of developments by following the news and official pronouncements, I could only imagine the carnage. It so happened that my guidebook was due for a reprint, so as soon as I got news of a new route avoiding the Cirque, I made plans to return and research it. That turned out to be one of the toughest walks of my life, but what else could I expect from Europe's toughest trail?

◀ The long descent from Bocca Crucetta to Refuge de Tighjettu

▽ The GR20 is steep, rocky and exposed near Pointe des Éboulis
   (photos: Paddy Dillon)

ARCTIC OCEAN

Denali ▲

ICELAND
Reykjavik ●

NORTH
AMERICA

New York ●

ATLANTIC
OCEAN

Mt. Whitney ▲

FRAN
COR
SPAI

MOROCCO
Marrakesh ▲
Toubkal

PACIFIC
OCEAN

SOUTH
AMERICA

Lima ●
PERU

Aconcagua ▲
Santiago ●

ARGENTINA

CHILE

Patagonia

SWEDEN

Stockholm

BALTIC
SEA

ASIA

EUROPE

Mont Blanc   Gora Elbrus
                              BLACK SEA   CASPIAN
                                                    SEA

GREECE

CRETE

Amman   JORDAN

Bishkek   KYRGYZSTAN

K2

Beijing

Kailash   CHINA

Manaslu

Islamabad   Mt Everest

PAKISTAN   BHUTAN

New   Kathmandu
Delhi

NEPAL

INDIA

FAR EAST

PACIFIC

OCEAN

AFRICA

Nairobi   KENYA

Mt Kilimanjaro

TANZANIA   Dar es Salaam

INDIAN

OCEAN

SOUTH   LESOTHO
AFRICA

Cape Town

AUSTRALIA

Canberra

Mt Kosciuszko   Wellington

Tasmania

Mt Cook

NEW ZEALAND

SOUTHERN OCEAN

Out there
ADVENTURES WORLDWIDE

There's a lot of 'out there' beyond Europe. There's the biggest, the highest, the steepest, the deepest, the hottest and coldest, the driest and the wettest. If you're in search of a new experience, you'll find a world of superlatives to fit the bill. It won't necessarily be a better or more lasting experience than it's possible to have at home – but it will be different. Very different. It will be more challenging, no doubt, because it is so far away from the familiar, with more opportunities for something to go badly wrong. That is the only guarantee when you're far from home: something will go wrong. Embrace the challenge of the unknown, and all that goes with it, for in that lies some of the romance, the appeal, and the very essence of adventure.

Here we have a bran tub of outdoor adventures on four different continents, played out among scenes full of mystery beyond the last blue horizon. To some they are the very stuff of dreams, told by those who have answered the call of the unknown, turned dreams into reality and discovered their very own Shangri-La. That's what guidebooks are for. They gather your dreams and show you how to transform them into reality. But the Shangri-La you find will be yours alone to cherish.

◄ The alternative Cape Pillar, Tasmania (photo: Ron Houghton)

34 The best way to Bou Guemez

HAMISH M BROWN

The French name for the Bou Guemez is La Vallée Heureuse (the happy valley). Apposite. Part of the lure for visitors is the near presence of 4068m Ighil Mgoun, the only 4000er in Morocco outwith the Toubkal massif, but the valley is a broad, well-watered paradise, with notable architecture and many gîtes to accommodate visitors. The valley today is reached by a west-flanking modern tarred road; earlier, a dramatic eastern dirt road climbed over to the Bou Guemez. I've always felt there was something missing, an experience demeaned, in simply driving in by the modern road. In 1986 we discovered the most befitting approach.

A friend and I took transport along the foothills eastwards from Marrakech to Azilal then on by a Bou Guemez lorry but, at Aït M'Hamid where the tarmac ended, we learned the pass ahead was blocked by snow. We could still walk a direct route that day, we were told. (Ah, we should have considered the Berber's rather relaxed views of time and distance.) We set off at noon, our ruckers on a hired mule, one of the boons of Atlas trekking.

We pulled up onto a vast plateau, polka-dotted with solitary trees. Rock buntings were the commonest birds, but crested larks were also sending their songs glissading down from overhead. There's a great lifting of the heart, a humbling, too, in finding such spaciousness. Hours on, topping a high crest, we stopped, awe-struck. The distant southern view was of snowy mountains (think Himalaya from Darjeeling), extensive enough to visibly dip, east and west, over the horizons. On subsequent visits, I've always enjoyed watching the faces of my companions on meeting that serendipitous shock – not one given to those sitting on their bums in a car.

The going became more complex. Hours passed. Time seemed elastic as we wended in and out of valleys and over ridges. At a bigger, greener valley, we had a second memorable experience. We had come to Sremt, a striking village dominated by a fortified house like a Scottish Borders tower, with narrow slits high on the walls and much herringbone-style decoration. A colourful Amazon ushered us in for mint tea and freshly baked bread – typical Berber hospitality. She put us on our way with an invitation to come again, to overnight, and that we happily did in years to come. With Sremt, the walk-in became a pleasant two-day trek that made the Bou Guemez seem like Shangri-La indeed.

⌃ A family home in Sremt, a striking village dominated by a fortified house

◁ A Berber shepherd boy of the Atlas Mountains
(photos: Hamish M Brown)

Hours on, we were ambushed for further refreshments, which we welcomed, for the day was hot, the ups and downs steeper and the miles lengthening. A woman in bright garments was watching a cow on a patch of cultivation; gamins, like pixies in their peaked djellaba hoods, came and kissed our hands. We heard a lot of singing and laughter, that mark of a contented people, satisfied with needs, not wants.

Eventually, off left, rose snowy Jbel Ouriat (c.3000m; climbed years later) and the dusk breeze off the snow soon chilled us. We swung round to the Tizi n' Aït Ouriat, the 2606m pass,

'A pleasant two-day trek that made the Bou Guemez seem like Shangri-La indeed'

where we were 1000m higher than our noon start. Darkness fell after a sunset of nuclear explosiveness, and a complex two and a half hours in pitch darkness led us down zigzags to the Bou Guemez. We came on juniper forest, then the sound of waters flowing, dogs barking, winking lights...

At the first house in the first village (Imelghas), I saw a brass plaque: 'Mohammed Achari, Guide de Montagne'. I hammered on the door. We had found La Vallée Heureuse, and the best, true way to gain it – and, in Mohammed, a great friend to be.

The summit of Jebel el Kest; the Sahara is not far away to the south

35 Exploring Morocco's Anti-Atlas

JONATHAN WILLIAMS

'Cicerone is all about exploring, and I really should do more of it, more of this...'

This was the thought I kept repeating to myself as we climbed higher through the dramatic rocks of Jebel el Kest, the highest peak in the region, one of many points on the 35km ridge that runs north of the small town of Tafraoute. The route Joe and I were on was rocky, with only occasional hints that there was a path, but the lie of the rocks, the naked geology, made our way clear as we climbed a broad ledge towards the summit.

The Anti-Atlas are just a four-hour flight away from rural Cumbria, but a world apart. Warm and dry, the Sahara is just a few kilometres to the south. Cumbria was dark, grey and cloudy as we left; here, it is clear, cool at night and nicely warm during the days. The glow of dawn comes on suddenly; and in the evenings, as we enjoy tagine and, surprisingly, wine in this relaxed Muslim country, the long, warm sunsets over the red mountains add a deeper glow.

The day had started with an incredible 10km drive up a dirt track, with a height gain of 1000m, to the remote hamlet of Anergui, and a walk through a narrow gap between the rocky mountains. Then came a long stretch during which we made our own route to a broad col, followed by the decision of whether to take the scramble up the ridge or the longer (but easier) walk round. For once, we took the easier way. From the summit shelter, we took in the immense views north to the High Atlas and south to the seemingly infinite hazy desert, while the muezzin issued the call to prayer from sleepy villages far below, unseen by and unknown to us.

We lingered, reluctant to leave. Joe pointed to a tiny pile of stones that might once have been a cairn. Ever curious, he set off to find out

98

what was below. After five minutes he returned: 'There's a route down – to somewhere.'

'Somewhere' was the west ridge of the mountain, a long narrow arête dropping steadily to unfamiliar ground. The route along the ridge was intricate, and we found gullies and nicks to help us negotiate the difficult terrain. Needing only the occasional steadying hand, it was rarely more than a walk, and an absolute delight to drop down through this hugely impressive mountain scenery. Clearly the route had existed for hundreds of years, known to the Berbers and local shepherds we were living among, but for us it was new, and for an hour we were explorers again.

The next day life changed suddenly. A tiny slip, nothing really, resulting in a destroyed quad tendon and a totally non-functioning leg, which left us rescuing ourselves from the remote mountains. Well, Joe was rescuing me. Adventures with the Moroccan medical system ensued, then a flight home, an ignominious trolley car through the airport and an operation in Lancaster. Immobilised for weeks and teaching my leg to walk again gave me the chance to look back on this trip and the other highlights of my time in the mountains and on the trails.

It was a period of rejuvenation, after which I would come back to exploring. I thought of the friendly villages of the Anti-Atlas, the fresh dates on sale in the market, the sunset glows, the incredible harsh terrain, the structured dance of buying a carpet – all of this I would come back to. I thought, too, of wild days in remote parts of Scotland, long climbs in snowy Alps, our 25th anniversary in an Alpine hut, the fellow feeling with pilgrims on the Camino, the brisk winds ever present on our local Howgills and the views to the bay, lakes and dreams of countries beyond.

And I thought of my rucksack, there in the back room, always packed and ready to go exploring.

'the sunset glows, the incredible harsh terrain, the structured dance of buying a carpet'

▽ Looking past the 'painted rocks' south of Toubkal in the early evening (photos: Jonathan Williams)

36 To climb Kilimanjaro

ALEX STEWART

I first came across photos of Kilimanjaro in my Kenya-born parents scrapbook, captured on expeditions they made across the border during the 1960s to climb the mountain in neighbouring Tanzania. In pictures of the glacier-capped colossus, Mawenzi's fearfully serrated talons shredded the skies; the rounded, snow-glazed brow of Kibo, a few miles away across a bleak lava plateau, stood higher still. I was smitten. The chance to follow in their footsteps and conquer Africa's contribution to the Seven Summits cemented my obsession.

Since then, independent trekking has been banned and climbing Kili has increased enormously in popularity. After all, where else on earth is it possible to scale a mountain of such a height without crampons, ice axes and a healthy fear of losing a few fingers to frostbite?

'That first, spine-tingling glimpse of the summit from the base camp on Kibo's flank'

Highlights from my first formative climb stay with me to this day: looking for colobus monkeys while trekking through cloud forest, marvelling at the remarkable senecio plants looming through the morning mist, crossing the alpine desert and camping among the lava bombs littering the upper slopes; speaking Swahili and singing with our crew of guides and porters, forming fast friendships, and that first, spine-tingling glimpse of the summit from the base camp on Kibo's flank; then waking at midnight below a clear, star-strewn sky for the assault on the insanely steep volcanic cone; my boots crunching on the hard ice, the bitter wind sucking the pathetic breath right out of my burning lungs as I struggled towards the crater rim, trying to beat the sun.

◄ Kibo/Kilimanjaro is a mesmerising sight across the saddle

▷ Sunrise colours the
summit glaciers
(photos: Alex Stewart)

Shuffle...pant, pant. Shuffle...pant, pant. One step. Two breaths. My guide constantly reminding me to go *pole, pole* (slowly, slowly). It's called the Kili Shuffle, and you can't refuse. Shuffle...pant, pant.

As one Kili biographer, John Reader, describes the final ascent: 'The climb is not difficult in mountaineering terms: you could say it was equivalent to climbing a staircase rather more than three kilometres long.' But when the staircase starts at 4600m, it's like climbing it with a sock stuffed in your mouth. 'The result is agonising. There is no other word for it.'

Eventually, I reached the rim of the world's largest volcano just as the sun burst from below the horizon and blazed into the heavens from behind the jagged, black form of Mawenzi. Below the Kersten, Heim and several other glaciers, the African savannah stretched away. There I stood, bent double, elation and pain battling for ascendancy among my emotions and gasping words. As people had warned, my head pounded like a tribal drum, I struggled to keep my nausea at bay, and my water froze in its bottle. The temperature sat at

> 'It's called the Kili Shuffle, and you can't refuse. Shuffle... pant, pant'

minus 20°C, while a buffeting wind tried to knock me off my feet and into the cauldron below to the right, or over one of the hanging glaciers to my left.

More painful still was the realisation that this point isn't even the top. It took a further two hours to skirt the 2km rim of Kibo to reach its highest point, Uhuru Peak, at 5895m. The whole summit looked unfinished. In the thin and freezing air, every line and every colour was sharp. Everything was jagged. There were no curves, no fading, no blurring. It was beautiful.

The climb could well be the toughest day of your life. But you'll be forever changed by it. Standing on the Roof of Africa, the sense of achievement I felt was almost as big as the mountain itself. I still get that incredible feeling. What's more, by walking slowly with my eyes open, I came home with something far more important than a summit certificate. Shuffle...pant, pant.

37 Sterkhorn

JEFF WILLIAMS

The southern Drakensberg mountains of South Africa can be a wild place. With areas where few people tread, an incident for a lone walker can be a major event. The 2973m Sterkhorn, in the Monk's Cowl area of 'the Berg' (as it is popularly known), is such a place. You don't need a rope for there's no technical climbing, but you do need stamina. It's a challenging walk, but a great one.

Starting from the Monk's Cowl main gate on a well-graded stony track, you pass landmarks with memorable names – Crystal Falls and the Sphinx – although in truth they are less dramatic than they sound. But Verkykerskop, Afrikaans for 'Far-looker's Hill', a regular dome when seen from the west, is a different matter. The top is only 70m above the path but looks a lot higher and the ascent track takes no prisoners in its directness. Sensible folk leave this fine viewpoint to consider on the return.

Now you reach the grassland plateau of the Little Berg, steep mountain slopes looming dramatically ahead. Here lies the Breakfast Stream, well known among wayfarers as a pleasant stopping place

for a snack and a drink. Like the rest of the Berg, it's potable water, if somewhat unreliable as a source, and a great place to see antelope if your approach is sufficiently discreet. I've seen reedbuck here and the hugely impressive eland, the largest of the African buck, weighing up to a hefty 600kg.

From here, you make fast progress westwards on a good path over easy terrain and, with the Sterkhorn directly ahead, reach the famous Blindman's Corner, a T-junction at the foot of the big mountains. The origin of this name is not entirely clear, although it has been suggested that it's such an obvious path junction that even a visually impaired person could find it.

This is where you leave the recognised tracks. A small path leads quickly to the first steep section. Really steep. Grassy too, so tough going. Clumps of grass for handholds don't work for me, but there's no danger. A bit further on, there's a short walk across a more exposed section that needs some care if the ground is wet and muddy. Now it feels more like a mountain, angling up across steep grass and a few

102

rocks, always traces of a path to breed confidence in your navigation. It's evident from the path that few travel this way and, on your own, the loneliness of the single walker in very high mountains may creep in. Some feel very insignificant and humble surrounded by such grandeur in a profoundly unfrequented place. For others, this is part of the exhilaration.

An awkward although mercifully short, steep and shallow gully of mud and grass leads up to a comfortable niche, a tiny col in reality. This is a good place to leave a ruck-sack, which is only a hindrance for the short climb to the summit cross. But take a drink and a snack to enjoy on the top. A scramble up easy

'Some feel very insignificant and humble surrounded by such grandeur in a profoundly unfrequented place'

rocks leads around the east face of the mountain, but then comes an apparent impasse. You are confronted by either a difficult rock climb up a narrow cleft, or a small cave, little above waist height. Neither are attractive. But be positive. Go underground (although if you've a very ample waistline, it will increase the challenge). Soon, light from above penetrates the darkness and you climb vertically, popping out like a conjuror's rabbit onto a very safe rocky platform. A final short and easy scramble takes you to the top.

The vista from here is what many people come for. For others, it's the scenic variety en route. For one or two of us, it's the challenge.

▽ Blindman's Corner looking south-west to Cathkin Peak
(photos: Jeff Williams)

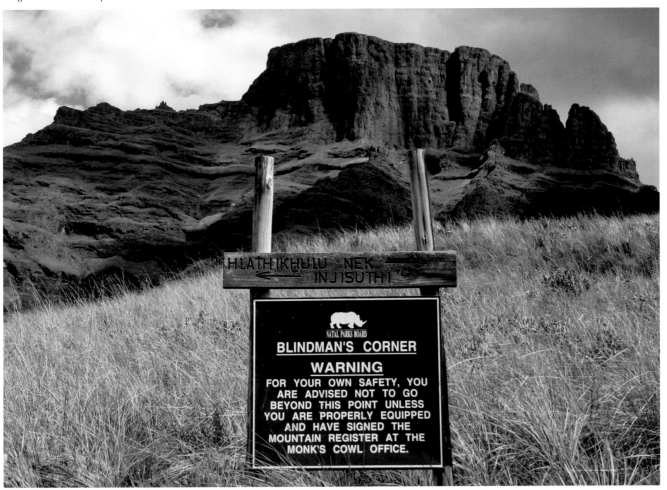

HLATHIKHULU NEK
INJISUTHI

NATAL PARKS BOARD
BLINDMAN'S CORNER
WARNING
FOR YOUR OWN SAFETY, YOU ARE ADVISED NOT TO GO BEYOND THIS POINT UNLESS YOU ARE PROPERLY EQUIPPED AND HAVE SIGNED THE MOUNTAIN REGISTER AT THE MONK'S COWL OFFICE.

38 The Jordan Trail

TONY HOWARD

Di Taylor and I have been exploring the mountains of Jordan since 1984. While researching routes for our trekking guide, we realised the potential for a 650km country-length trail, mostly along hills forming the eastern rim of Jordan's Rift Valley. Almost 20 years of annual spring visits were to pass before it was completed with local friends. The Jordan Trail Association was then formed to develop and promote it for the benefit of the country.

What a superb trek it is, best walked in springtime when springs flow with water and the flowers are in bloom – not just in the green forested hills of the north, but in the Dead Sea canyons and the deserts of the south. By 2017, homestays had been established, wild campsites located, and local guides and drivers trained, enabling us to enjoy the trek while equipment was transported ahead.

Heading south, the first six days pass through flower-filled meadows and forests of Mediterranean oak and strawberry trees, with Muslim and Christian villages and their orchards and olive groves. The trail also passes Greco-Roman antiquity sites, ruins of ancient churches and the hilltop Islamic fortress of Ajlun Castle. Here, the trail is often on

'Best walked in springtime when springs flow with water and the flowers are in bloom'

established paths or country lanes over rolling hills, with views across the sub-sea-level, verdant Jordan Valley to the distant hills of Palestine. Another eight days cross hills incised by wadis tumbling into the Jordan Valley. Overnighting in the Christian town of Fuheis, we enjoy Carakale beer from the local brewery, and in the Women's Cooperative of Iraq al-Amir, with its Hellenistic palace, home-cooked food and accommodation.

Next come the three great canyons that carve their way to the Dead Sea, more than 400m below sea level. All are between 800 and 1000m deep and, as ever in Jordan, local Bedouin know the way. Excellent trails descend and ascend past dolmens and Bedouin camps, with the usual invitation to drink tea and stay for a meal. And how refreshing to plunge hot feet into the rivers!

A week later, the trail reaches the mighty Crusader castle of Karak before continuing to another giant canyon, Wadi Hasa, with its hot springs. Petra is the following week's destination, after overnighting first in the idyllic clifftop villages of Ma'tan, then Dana in Jordan's largest nature reserve, before descending to lunch in the Feynan Ecolodge in Wadi Araba, the southern extension of Jordan's Rift Valley. Another Bedouin trail leaves the hot, arid terrain, climbing dramatically to the heights of Wadi Feid. It then follows the escarpment rim along a Nabatean trail shown to us by Bedouin back in the early 1990s, arriving in Petra through its 'back door'.

From Petra, one of the New Seven Wonders of the World and, like Wadi Rum, a World Heritage Site, we follow Bedouin trails for another week through dramatic desert mountain country almost devoid of water, to reach the day-long canyon of Aheimir. Then the desert plateau extends to the mountains of Wadi Rum, described by TE Lawrence as 'magnificent...vast, echoing and godlike' – our climbing playground every spring for 30 years.

A final week remains. We walk through the maze of Rum's desert valleys on orange sand between striated sandstone cliffs, before finally crossing two passes in Aqaba's granite coastal mountains to see the Red Sea far below, turquoise and tempting. Our hot feet speed us down the last sandy wadi and into the welcoming waves.

⌃ A lone trekker is dwarfed by the walls of the Aheimir Canyon

◁ Trekking through Petra on the Jordan Trail
(photos: Tony Howard)

39 Kyrgyzstan's Tian Shan

MADELINE WILLIAMS

Halfway up a winding green valley, where slate crags shone blue under the rain and our horses shook spatters of droplets from sodden manes, we came upon the ancient Silk Road caravanserai Tash Rabat. The high walls and dome rose stern and strange from the side of the valley, and wandering those ancient halls we could not help but imagine the refuge that centuries of travellers had found there. The following day, the outlook couldn't have been more different; storms segued into blue skies, the fresh green of the valley gave way to high screes like rumpled

velvet, and like innumerable caravans before us we made a chain-link of horses climbing up into the heights of the Tian Shan to reach the first view of China.

The sheer wildness combined with the variety of mountain architecture is why Kyrgyzstan's central Tian Shan, and this route, are favourites. Riding day after day from the high-altitude lake of Son Kul south through ravines, desert canyons and rolling Yorkshire-like uplands, this adventure with Wild Frontiers had a feeling of authenticity much like walking a pilgrim route; you know this is how the trek must be travelled.

A highlight – and high point – of the route was the long climb from Tash Rabat to Chatyr-Kul. We set off towards a forbidding wall of rock and ice, somewhere close to 5000m. Our path flitted over a river and climbed craggy hillsides that dropped sharply into a river-cut gorge. We skirted to the side of the icy cliffs, and the 4100m pass was before us: grey and grim after our time in the desert and green valleys. We donned layers for the climb; although it was August, we'd left the heat behind us, days away and thousands of metres below. The path was long and sheer, our horses dug hooves into the shifting scree, heads down, and made their way ever upwards. Breathless from altitude, and with the strong wind blasting out of the north, we had our first view of the other side; it was desolate and empty, yet achingly beautiful. The route dropped sharply down on scree before giving way to grassy hills that piled together, crag-crested like waves, rolling into a plain and down to a large lake. The clouds scudding above cast shadows on the watercolour blue of Chatyr-Kul, stretching with a mirror sheen below a sentinel line of high white peaks that guarded a natural border with China.

Many hours of riding later, we made camp tucked into the lee of a cliff. Once the sun fled behind a hill, the temperature plummeted and everything we had with us was thrown on and zipped up as the stars

'It was desolate and empty, yet achingly beautiful'

came out. That far from anything approaching light pollution, the sky was lit up, the stars blushing in a Milky Way smear across the gap from hill to hill. We lay back and looked, huddled on horse blankets and clutching mugs of tea, and it was almost as if you could step out into the black and find yourself surrounded by the pinpricked light.

It doesn't take long to fall happily into the life of riding every day, finding new sights over every hill. Turning away from that, from the mountains and our new Kyrgyz friends back to a more complicated life, felt too soon in coming. We would have been happy to carry on, or at least plan to come back. And surely that's a sign of a great trek; that odd reverse-homesickness where you look around these strange and wonderful places, and promise yourself that you'll be back.

◁ Climbing the high pass to Chatyr-Kul

▽ Chatyr-Kul and the border range
(photos: Madeline Williams)

40 The Leslie–Karamea Track

GRANT BOURNE

In autumn, the afternoon sun does not penetrate the narrow valley through which the Cobb Dam road twists, losing itself in ever deepening shadow. There is no exit for this road which, after a laborious climb to the Cobb Reservoir, can only peter out as if spent before the vastness of New Zealand's Kahurangi National Park. The only way onward is on foot, some 86km through rugged wilderness to the West Coast of the South Island at Little Wanganui.

On its way to the coast, this difficult but exhilarating trail leads past an abandoned asbestos mine and a former gold prospector's cottage, deep into the golden tussock country of the Mount Arthur Tablelands. From there it descends through mossy, and often dripping,

native beech forest to the Leslie and Karamea rivers. A string of huts provide welcome refuge along the way, but it is necessary to carry your own supplies and a portable stove.

Although it has been some time since I did the walk, the impressions it made on me remain vivid. I can still hear the song of the bellbirds that accompanied us as we navigated mist-hung river valleys, and the heavy swish of air in the forest canopy, betraying the laboured flight of a wood pigeon. Along the track, we often encountered one of New Zealand's flightless birds, the almost tame weka.

All treks (known as tramps in New Zealand) seem to contain at least one thoroughly soggy day when the veil of mist which hangs gloomily

Drowned trees poke eerily from the waters of Moonstone Lake, formed by an earthquake-triggered slip

After finally reaching the west coast, the reward is a magnificent sunset

over the valley refuses to budge and an emphatic downpour confirms the sun's banishment. Wispy streams are swollen in minutes, gushing down precipitous slopes and adding to the river's roar. But on the plus side, the bush is very beautiful, as the dampness serves to accentuate the emerald greens or the occasionally bright splotch of a violet pouch fungus along the way.

However, rain can also signify danger on lonely backcountry trails. After leaving one hut, we had to ford a swollen creek and the track from then on bore many similarities to a stream. At one point, where it followed closely the banks of the flooded Karamea, it disappeared underwater and we had to scramble through steep bush slopes before we could descend to it again. On a greasy boulder, I overbalanced with my heavy pack and fell, gashing my left knee on the rock – to my relief I could still walk reasonably well. Venus Hut came as a welcome sight and we thankfully dropped our packs in this haven of shelter.

Nothing pleases drenched trampers more than dry firewood and a good fire. Venus was blessed with both. It continued to pour outside,

'Nothing pleases drenched trampers more than dry firewood and a good fire'

but with our mugs of soup and fresh clothes we were gratefully indifferent. My leg grew very stiff and swollen, so the collection of old magazines in the hut were thoroughly read as we had to remain an extra day.

The weather barely improved as we slogged our way along muddy tracks, passing the beautiful and eerie Moonstone Lake and fording Kendall Creek before arriving at Trevor Carter Hut. After a night spent there, we continued to Taipo Hut and then Little Wanganui Hut, where we spent the last two nights of our trek to the coast.

It took us eight days to accomplish what is one of New Zealand's most beautiful and varied walks. The entire tramp could be done in less time, but an even more leisurely pace would do it more justice. This trip is the closest most people will get to appreciating the efforts of John Rochford and Thomas Salisbury, the early explorers of the region, while the superb huts and track enable anyone who is fit to conduct their own exploration in the most intimate way possible – on foot.

Sub-tropical vegetation adds variety to the last leg of the tramp
(photos: Grant Bourne)

A The Blade and Tasman Island

41 The Three Capes Track

ROB HOUGHTON

On the third day of our hike in south-east Tasmania, looming out of the haar, we caught our first glimpse of Cape Pillar. More colloquially known as the Blade, it was the second of the eponymous three capes and by far the most spectacular. The Blade, a shark's fin of dolerite, juts defiantly out into the sea. With Tasman Island to its south, it forms a dramatic exclamation point on the end of the continent. South of here, there is nothing until you reach Antarctica and, standing on the ridge, there is nothing but ocean to either side of you. It is bleak and forbidding and not a little hair-raising. If you have the nerve and are used to scrambling, it's possible to stand on the very end of this peninsula and imagine the unimaginable hardship of the keepers of the lighthouse just beyond you.

> 'It feels like the edge of the world'

It feels like the edge of the world.

It's not all existential contemplation on the Three Capes Track, however. A four-day hike along the southern coast of Tasmania, it feels at times like the island in microcosm. Tasmania has something of a reputation among the rest of the Australian states and territories. It is generally held to be halfway between a gothic horror location and a rural backwater, akin to both Wuthering Heights and Worzel Gummidge. In truth, it is achingly beautiful and has, in recent years, capitalised on that natural abundance.

The Three Capes, the latest of Tazzie's long-distance hikes, is a case in point. The walk begins, as does the colony's history, with a convict settlement. Port Arthur was originally built to be the latest thing in humane convict rehabilitation. However, it quickly became hated and feared by the convicts for the horrors that they had to face there. Today a World Heritage Site, it is a serene park that hides a brutal past, and is the dropping-off point for the walk.

From the penitentiary to Fortescue Bay it is 45km of walking. Along the way, you'll pass sea cliffs, stands of tea tree, historical sites and moorland. At one point, you'll even descend into a section of temperate cloud forest, which will send you scurrying for your spare layer. There is a fabulous array of wildlife and you may be lucky enough to spot wallabies, echidnas, possums, wombats or quolls – a roll-call of the exotic to European ears. And every so often, there is a place to rest and a chapter of the accompanying guidebook to help you interpret what you're seeing. It really is Tasmania in miniature, the only thing missing being the wineries.

It is not a short walk, and there are uphills and steep descents. You pass through places called Hurricane Heath and Perdition Ponds, which hint at how remote this peninsula was until very recently. And, importantly, you have to carry all your food with you as there are no porters here; but it is nonetheless a very civilised sort of adventure. The trail is very well maintained and impossible to lose, and each night is spent in relative luxury. The three purpose-built huts in which you cook and sleep have won design awards. Although they are built from steel and wood, they seem to rise organically from their surroundings and provide a comforting end to each day.

So long as you have remembered to pack a bag of wine, it is pure bliss to return, unscathed, from the very edge of the world and watch the sun descend over the sea with a glass of Tasmanian red in your hand.

▽ Overnight accommodation is in three purpose-built huts
(photos: Rob Houghton)

42 Tippex on the summit of the Americas

JIM RYAN

It was the year 2000 when I made my first attempt on Aconcagua, having joined a group of 13 on an expedition from Ireland. These included an Irish expedition leader, an Argentinean guide and an assistant guide. Of the ten 'clients', there were some who, in hindsight, had no chance of summiting, but six or seven were quite capable, although our first doubt about the guide was when we replaced him as pacesetter, because he was going too fast.

> 'I had brought a stone from Carrauntoohil in Ireland to place on the summit'

The weather on summit day could not have been better. When we arose, the temperature was just a few degrees below zero. We left one of our group behind at Camp Berlin (5850m) and another had to

abandon below Independencia at an altitude of 6400m. At Cresto del Viento (6550m), the guide and the expedition leader began to talk. The guide had not expected so many of us to get this far. He would take the expedition leader and a maximum of four others to the summit. The rest would have to descend with the assistant guide. If he had complied with the recommended ratio of a guide (or assistant guide) to every two, or maximum three, clients, then more would have been able to proceed.

To my utter astonishment, I was told I would be one of those to retreat. There, at 6550m, I had a heated argument with the expedition leader. It was 10.30am, with little wind and not a cloud in the sky. I felt

good and strong. The summit was two hours away, so initially I decided to proceed on my own.

'I am the expedition leader and I am ordering you to descend. If you proceed you do so on your own, bearing your own risks.'

In hindsight, I should have ignored that order, but I descended, shattered and deeply troubled at the injustice of it all. When I reflect on it, even now, what had been inflicted on me was the worst let-down of my entire life. A year preparing, thousands of pounds spent, two weeks' trekking, and I could not summit – not because I was incapable, not because of the weather, but because, as I later discovered, the guide was not registered, and had not undergone the requisite training to lead at altitude. He was just another climber.

I had brought a stone from Carrauntoohil in Ireland to place on the summit of Aconcagua. On it I had written, in Tippex, 'From Carrauntoohil, Ireland'. I left it behind at the Independencia Hut.

The next year I was back, but this time with an experienced and competent Argentinean guide whom I had carefully sourced, and together we trekked up the longer Vacas Valley route. Conditions on the mountain were vastly different from the year before. On the morning of our summit day, the temperature outside the tent was minus 35°C, the wind chill accounting for 20°C of that. At the summit, it was minus 25°C. It was a constant problem between getting precious air and protecting our faces from the wind – what a tragedy to have missed the opportunity on that warm day a year before!

At Independencia, I found my stone, still with the Tippex writing fully legible, and carried it to the summit. Now there are two stones from Ireland lying there...

43 In search of Alpamayo

KEV REYNOLDS

On Sunday 31 May 1970, Peru suffered a major earthquake. Standing 150km from the epicentre, Huascarán, the country's highest mountain, shuddered like an enormous blancmange. Moments later, the west face of the north peak shed an estimated 15 million cubic metres of rock and ice which, along with a mass of glacial silt, mud and snow, sped towards the town of Yungay. Within three minutes, the town and 18,000 of its inhabitants ceased to exist.

Thirty years later I thought of that mind-numbing tragedy as I, along with a small group of trekkers and a team of Quechua Indians and their burros, crossed a pass 'behind' that mountain of betrayal as we went in search of Alpamayo.

Although Alpamayo, once voted the world's most beautiful mountain, was the focus of our quest, the haunting spirit of Huascarán was seldom far away. Yet each day we trekked through avenues of exquisite mountains, peaks of the Cordillera Blanca whose names I struggled to work my tongue around – names like Taulliraju, Chacraraju, Chopicalqui, Huandoy and Pucahirca. We crossed passes almost 5000m high, and wandered through valleys as green and homely as Borrowdale. We watched in awe as avalanches poured down the face of mountains just out of reach, camped on tussocks of wiry grass and were nearly blown off our feet when breaking camp one wild and inhospitable morning.

> Alpamayo is reflected in a
> shallow pool near our camp

< Alpamayo, once voted the
world's most beautiful
mountain
(photos: Kev Reynolds)

Of all the world's mountains, these Andean giants had a unique appeal. I'd peer from my tent most mornings before first light, and wait for the magic of daybreak to spill its colours onto glaciers that seemed to hang suspended from nothing but crests of meringue. I'd never seen ice like it and was glad to be a mere trekker with no desire to climb what looked so insanely fragile. Fragile, yes, but so utterly beautiful – especially when seen through a frieze of exotic plants visited by birds I'd never before set eyes on.

Every day was a treat for all my senses. But where was Alpamayo?

On the eighth day, we fought our way across one of the highest passes of the trek, and descended into a bullying wind that tossed clouds of dust and even small stones at us. The previous night we'd camped in a moonscape of rocks and little vegetation, but now we had a more welcoming sight before us – a valley full of promise, walled by mountains whose summits had been levelled and carried

'Every day was a
treat for all my
senses. But where
was Alpamayo?'

off by banks of cloud. But there was hope in the mystery those clouds imposed, and I felt sure that when they parted they would reveal what we'd been searching for.

We pitched our tents in a meadow sliced by a torrent whose voice would be silenced by a double glazing of ice when the sun went down.

A bitter chill gripped the camp, and, as evening drew in, first a squall of rain then hail hammered against the ageing tent fabric. It didn't last long, so I pulled on my down jacket and crawled outside to see the burros, now free of their loads, rolling on their backs in a patch of sand-like glacier flour. Nearby, a fox with a blue-grey coat and a long tail was nosing among the rocks.

Then I looked up and my mouth went dry. There was Alpamayo at last. Clouds had swept aside and she was revealed in all her glory – a perfect cone of rock, snow and ice standing sentry-like at the head of the valley. Alpamayo! I stood bewitched by a sublime vision of glory as my eyes began to water. But not from the cold.

44 The Inca Trail

WILL JANECEK

A road, in perfect harmony with its rugged surroundings, makes a four-day physical and spiritual journey to one of the Seven Wonders of the World. Endless kilometres of intricately laid, wide stone paths climb up and over high-altitude mountain passes on massive stairways carved into the side of sheer walls of granite.

These are features of the incredible trail-building skills of the Incas: playful, suspenseful, and ambitious; a combination of arrogance and excellence, of pride and determination, and physical endurance; the masterful tying together of earth, stone, mountain, river and sky in a manner which can only be described by the word 'art'.

Superlatives? Not to anyone who has ever hiked the Inca Trail to Machu Picchu, that 99km paved stairway through the steep Andes Mountains of Peru. This royal road features countless waterfalls and mountain viewpoints, crosses four passes over 3600m high, and winds through no less than two dozen Inca buildings, palaces and outposts before arriving dramatically at its final destination.

Built well over 650 years ago, the Inca Trail may be a misnomer, as there are an estimated 25,000 miles (40,000km) of Inca-built or enhanced roadways, stretching from Chile to Ecuador. Unlike other road systems such as those of the Romans, Egyptians and other civilisations, Inca roads were never meant to accommodate the wheel

◁ Machu Picchu, one of the Seven
Wonders of the World

▷ The Inca Trail teeters along dramatically steep
mountainsides
(photos: Will Janecek)

– the incredibly steep and jagged topography of the Andes simply did not allow for it. However, this freed the Incas to build dramatic roads straight up and over mountains and along ridgelines – which they did so effectively.

Built in the 1400s as a vacation estate for Incan royalty, Machu Picchu, as far as we know, was never discovered by the Spanish invaders. The trail to it was more than just a route of transit; it was an experience, a cleansing ritual, a higher level of meaning.

Typically the Inca Trail involves four days of hiking and three nights of camping, beginning at the Km 82 checkpoint on the Urubamba River, then following the Kusichaka River to Wayllabamba, where it heads west, deep into the Andes. Climbing through the cloud forest and native *Polylepis* trees, it passes a campsite called Llulluch'apampa before reaching its highest point at a 4215m pass.

The trail reaches a second pass at 3950m, then passes a beautifully built outpost, Sayaqmarka (steep-place town), and a long, dramatic Inca tunnel, before gaining a view of the confluence of two important rivers far below.

'After climbing
the final set of
steps, you arrive
at a scene you will
never forget'

Soon the third pass, at 3652m, is crossed, then there appears Phuyupatamarka (cloud-level town), a magnificent Incan complex with many water fountains. After this comes a staircase of approximately 1500 steps, carved into the solid granite face. As you descend, the jungle appears with its flowers, colourful birds and lush vegetation.

The Inca Trail passes stunning Wiñay Wayna with its many fountains, offering the opportunity for a final cleanse, then undulates along below the crest of the east slope of the mountain named Machu Picchu. The steep false-summit stairs leading to Inti Punku (Quechuan for 'sun gate') are reached at last, and after climbing the final set of steps, you arrive at a scene you will never forget.

Only those who have hiked the Inca Trail will ever know the exhilaration that comes from that first glimpse of Machu Picchu. Sometimes famous places don't meet expectations. But trekking for four days through very rugged terrain to arrive here at Inti Punku and look down the grand staircase to Machu Picchu – this is one of those rare experiences that not only meets but far exceeds anything you could possibly have imagined.

45 The Torres del Paine Circuit

RUDOLF ABRAHAM

The beauty of the landscape in Chile's iconic Torres del Paine National Park, in the remote wilds of southern Patagonia, is staggering. Vertical spires of granite tower above a landscape of primeval forest, turquoise lakes and vast sheets of ice. Rock faces glow blood red in the first few moments of early morning light, condors circle in the skies above, and at night the silence is broken by the guttural moan of glaciers.

The Torres del Paine Circuit, or the 'O', as it's often called, is an epic hiking route through some of the most alluring mountain scenery imaginable. It passes close to the iconic Torres (towers) after which the park is named, as well as above and alongside the awe-inspiring expanse of Glaciar Grey; below the distinctive Cuernos (horns), and through beautiful forests of Antarctic beech, Magellanic coigüe and lenga. It takes around ten days to complete – ten days of the kind of hiking which will remain etched on the back of your mind forever.

On my first visit to Patagonia I hiked the southern part of the route – the 'W', as it's also known – after spending several days in Los Glaciares National Park, just over the border in Argentina. On that visit to Torres del Paine, I remember gazing awestruck across the Rio Francés at the huge east face of Cerro Paine Grande, as it caught the early morning sun, its glaciers glittering and framed by spectral clouds. The following year I returned to hike the Circuit, heading north then west alongside the headwaters of the Rio Paine to Lago Dickson; past Glaciar Los Perros, its surface bristling with seracs the size of houses; then up to the bleak, rock-strewn saddle that is Paso John Gardner, the highest point on the route at an altitude of only 1180m – although the wind up here can make it almost impossible to stand.

> 'An epic hiking route through some of the most alluring mountain scenery imaginable'

It's hard to name a favourite spot, a view of all views, on this route. There are simply too many of them. The picture-postcard views of the Cuernos across Lago Nordenskjöld, or of the Torres illuminated at dawn, are often the ones which first lure people to Patagonia. But then there's the view along the skyline of sabre-toothed peaks above the Valle Francés – Cerro Espada (the spear), and Cerro Fortaleza. And that first sight of Glaciar Grey from the crest of Paso John Gardner is unforgettable. The sheer immensity of it takes your breath away – some 6km across at this point, its fractured surface streaked with blue. Yet despite its scale, it is effectively just a sliver of ice spewing out from the edges of the enormous Campo de Hielo Sur, the largest sheet of ice in the southern hemisphere outside Antarctica.

I've never managed to spot that most iconic of big cats, the elusive puma. But I've seen plenty of other wildlife in and around the national park – guanaco sauntering across a hillside, ibis wading through a carpet of flowers, torrent ducks perched on water-bound rocks in the silent, upper reaches of the Valle Ascensio. Once, stumbling up a steep-sided trail in screaming winds, I turned to see a condor being swept upwards beside me, motionless except for the tips of its wings, and so close I felt I could almost reach out and touch it.

Despite the popularity of the route – to the extent that several new regulations were introduced at the end of 2016, intended to reduce overcrowding on the trails – the landscape feels no less wild, especially along the northern stretch, and hiking the Torres Circuit remains a hugely rewarding experience, on one of the world's truly great treks.

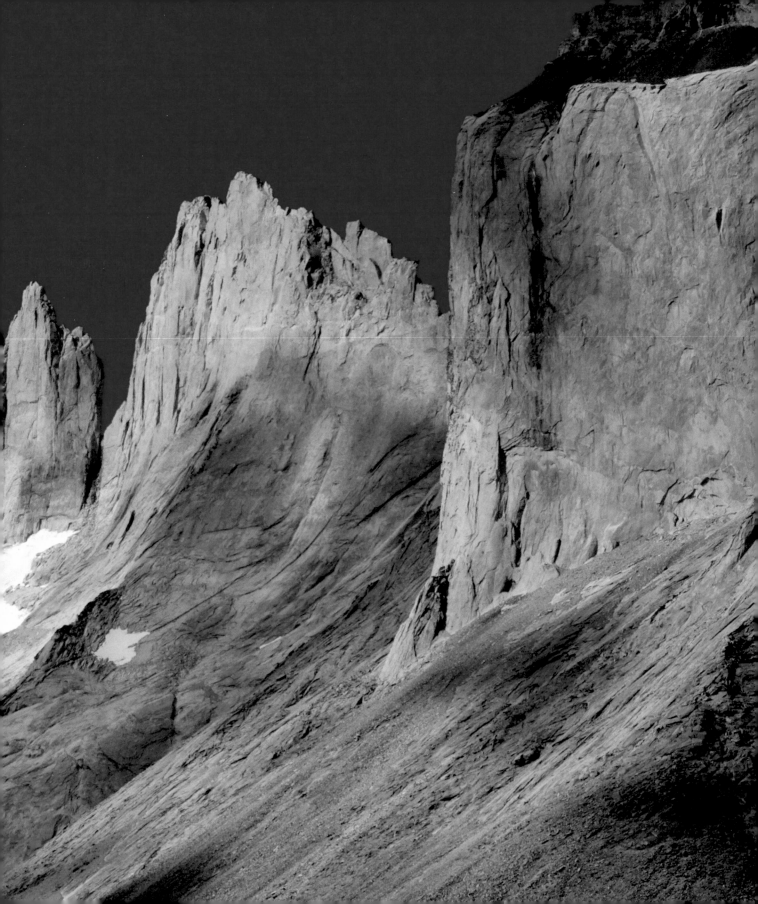

46 The Lunana Snowman Trek

BART JORDANS

Hidden in a secluded recess high in the Himalayan mountains of northern Bhutan, Lunana forms the heart of what many experienced trekkers consider to be one of the longest, hardest and most beautiful of all treks. Imposing snow-capped peaks, seemingly impassable river gorges and mammoth glaciers isolate its villages from the outside world, the only access being via steep and rocky high-altitude trails. With 14 lofty passes to cross and several camps at around 5000m, the four-week Snowman Trek may be compared to three Everest Base Camp treks in succession.

Tucked between Tibet and India, the small, predominantly Buddhist nation of Bhutan is lanced by deep ravines and coated with dense woodland – more than 70 per cent of the country is covered by forest. Flying over the kingdom reveals both human habitation and large empty pockets of land, promising a varied trek of days with and without human contact. But visiting and sometimes camping in the villages is a real delight, since some of the more remote communities reveal a unique cultural heritage.

The endless grandeur of the scenery, the villages and people met along the way, days of remoteness, the length of the journey, its connections with Buddhism and nature, walking beside unclimbed 7000m peaks that form the border with Tibet – all these things and more make this my all-time favourite trek. Even after guiding in Bhutan since 1994 and having lived there for four and a half years, each time I land at Paro airport is like entering a dream. Embraced by the sweet, clean mountain air, eyes focus on the immaculate scenery – hills dotted with beautiful decorated farmhouses, and one of the huge *dzongs* (fortified monasteries) for which the country is famed.

After spending time in the Paro Valley, our long adventure begins. Supported by local guides and staff who provide excellent food throughout the trek, legs get their long-awaited exercise as we wander close to the border with Tibet, where several passes are still being used for illegal trade. Chinese goods such as solar panels, rubber boots, Tibetan ponies, cigarettes and alcohol find their way into Bhutan, while travelling in the opposite direction, wood products, incense, Indian goods and highly valued cordyceps pass into Tibet.

After two or three days' hiking, we draw close to some huge Himalayan peaks, including Jhomolhari (7315m), climbed in 1937 by Freddie Spencer Chapman and Pasang Dawa Lama, and the pointy mountain Jitchu Drake (c.6800m) nearby. But all Bhutanese peaks are now out of bounds – many years ago a ban was put on climbing here in order to avoid disturbing the spirits that dwell among the summits.

After the first of the 14 high passes, we come to three beautiful and authentic villages – Lingshi, Goyok and Chebisa – then there are more remote days before we reach the next group of villages around Laya. An extra day is used to explore Laya itself before venturing onwards for Lunana, which begins after we cross one of the highest passes of the trek – the Karakachu La (5020m). Once we've entered the Lunana area, there are only high passes left to exit!

Lunana is the trek's undisputed highlight, with another couple of villages to visit among even more impressive mountain scenery. And it is not finished yet – from the heart of Lunana there are two equally wild exits of six or seven days to the nearest road. For me, these represent the trek's crowning glory, being almost without habitation but with wild nature and views to some amazing mountains like the highest of them all – Gankar Punsum (7541m).

Tashi Delek!

> 'The endless grandeur of the scenery, the villages and people..., days of remoteness'

▲ Gankar Punsum, Bhutan's highest mountain at 7541m, seen here from near the Gophu La
(photos: Bart Jordans)

▲ The magnificent north and east faces of Mount Kailash

47 The heaven and hell of Mount Kailash

SIÂN PRITCHARD-JONES AND BOB GIBBONS

*The power of such a mountain is so great and yet so subtle
that, without compulsion, people are drawn to it from near
and far, as if by the force of some invisible magnet...*

The Way of the White Clouds, **Lama Anagarika Govinda**

Hindus worship Mount Kailash in Tibet as the abode of the god Shiva. Buddhists circle it to cleanse themselves of sin. Followers of Bon and Jainism revere it equally. William Moorcroft was the first Englishman to see the mountain, but he visited as a spy during the Great Game. We

claim no such motivations other than to gaze on this exotic, remote peak in Shangri-La, and to survive the journey.

Just getting to Mount Kailash involves an epic road journey from Kathmandu. The effects of altitude inevitably play mind games for the first few days. We nearly abandon the trek when a snowstorm intervenes; it is so cold in the hotel in Saga that we need to sit under an infrared lamp in the bathroom to keep warm.

Our budget 'pot noodle trek' begins from Darchen, where people huddle beside fire hearths in stone houses waiting for the sun to burst forth. It's late in the season; only a few Tibetan pilgrims accompany

124

us on the trail. The guide is quite disinterested but the two porters are magnificent stalwarts.

We hike north along an eerie canyon passing strange defiles to the east, where Kailash grants a glimpse of its snow-covered ramparts. After Chuku Monastery are the peaks of Tara, Amitayus and Vijeya, the icons of longevity – longevity in this place! A golden sunset catches the face of Kailash at Driraphuk Monastery; it's a magical moment to lift the spirits to unworldly heights. After pot noodles and on hard beds, little sleep follows.

The north faces of Kailash are staggeringly sheer, painted by icy fingers like the tentacles of a white spider. We trudge on up at an imperceptible pace; it's a battle to keep to a rhythm. We pass a meadow littered with old clothes. This is Shiwal Tsal, the place of the dead, where the gods decide a person's fate. Pilgrims offer discarded clothing; others lie down as if feigning death. We just lie down exhausted.

The Drolma La (5660m) is the only pass on the route. For the pilgrims, it's a joy, as one's sins wash away, but for foreign devils it's a bit of

'Exhausting, exciting, arduous and intoxicating – a high altitude merry-go-round of heaven and hell'

a torment. The pass proves exhausting, exciting, arduous and intoxicating – a high altitude merry-go-round of heaven and hell. The descent is rocky, passing a sacred pond, menaced by darkness and ice. Lower down, we encounter a nomad tent; boisterous Tibetans, wrapped in yak-skin coats, have a brew on. It's a godsend, but the tea is Tibetan, a mix of rancid butter and milky tea. Even this concoction is welcomed.

Rugged multi-coloured crags and snowy spires grace the trail to Zutrulphuk Monastery. Another bitter night has to be endured on plank beds after a meal of muesli and English Breakfast tea. Sunrise is rejuvenating. The trail back to Darchen is as easy as ambling around the 'Kentish Alps'; a cloud of euphoria accompanies us.

As for Moorcroft, he was convinced that Russian envoys had been in Tibet. Curiously, he based his opinion on the presence of two European-bred dogs in a Tibetan village. It was hardly compelling evidence.

▼ Driraphuk Monastery on the Mount Kailash trek
(photos: Siân Pritchard-Jones)

Emerging from the Buri Gandaki's gorge, the first clear view of Manaslu is gained from the village of Lhogaon

48 The Manaslu Circuit

KEV REYNOLDS

An hour's hike above Gorkha, that historic Nepalese township between Kathmandu and Pokhara, you come onto a ridge to be confronted by a view to make your heart leap. There, across a terraced land of rice and millet dotted with mud-coloured thatched houses, a great wall of mountains spreads across your field of vision: the Manaslu Himal ahead, Annapurnas to the left, Ganesh Himal to the right. If ever there was a landscape of perfection, this is it. Four times I've gazed on that view with misted eyes, but it's invaded my dreams at least a hundred times more.

Around that central block of mountains runs the Manaslu Circuit, a three-week journey among tiny villages open to the sun, and through deep-shadowed gorges sliced by the most thunderous of rivers. There are waterfalls pouring from notches cut in the sky. There are fields of barley below glaciers spilling from some of the highest mountains on earth. There are *kanis* (entrance archways) decorated with Buddhist motifs to pass through, and *gompas* (Buddhist monasteries) from whose sacred rooms echo unfathomable prayers. In the high country, yak graze the

> 'This is wild nature at its very best – a Genesis land, fresh and untamed'

pastures, lammergeier haunt the thermals and every lofty summit offers a benediction.

It'll take us ten days or so to cross the foothills, penetrate the gorges and emerge under Manaslu's gaze. But what days they are! Every half-hour is different. I love wandering the foothill country, for this is rural Nepal at its best – the beating heart of the land. So we pad our way across the low hills, enter the valley of the Buri Gandaki at Arughat Bazar, and then head north alongside the river, which we'll cross and recross a dozen times or more before we leave its company below the Tibetan border, and make for the Larkya La.

Our highest village is Samdo, built from nothing by Tibetan refugees who fled the Chinese invasion in the 1950s. We camp there two or three nights, not just to acclimatise, but to savour its atmosphere and the beauty of its views. Gazing down-valley we have Manaslu and its neighbours soaring up and up as if to support the sky on their summits. Behind the village, an abrupt hill getting on for 5000m makes an amazing viewpoint, with our eyes naturally focused on the high pass that is the crux of our route, just two days away.

Last time I crossed the 5135m Larkya La, I cheated. My lungs, wrecked from historic damage, I knew I'd not make it on two legs, so chose four. A Samdo woman let me ride her horse for a day and a half until the snow was too deep to continue. So I slid off the saddle (a wooden one whose scars I can still feel when I sit), staggered alone to the pass, and sat in the snow among the prayer flags to wait for my group.

Descent to the Bimtang meadow is always a tangle of weariness and sheer exhilaration. But long after the weariness has been forgotten, it's the immense panorama that stays in the mind. Mountains, snow-fields, gullies, glaciers and glacial moraines fill every view. This is wild nature at its very best – a Genesis land, fresh and untamed, into which it's a great privilege to stray.

Two days later, we join the Annapurna Circuit and trek down the Marsyangdi to Bhulbhule, then cut away into the land of rice once more, exchanging the known way for narrow paths on dykes between paddies on a return to Gorkha – a mind-blowing contrast to the days of snow and ice we've just left behind. In such contrasts lie the joys of trekking.

▼ A makeshift bridge carries the trail across a tributary of the Buri Gandaki
(photos: Kev Reynolds)

49 To Zanskar along the Tsarab Chu

RADEK KUCHARSKI

'Did you carry your rucksack above your head while crossing the Tsarab River?' a man from the British group asked me. We had met three days earlier in Tsokmitsik. The group, led by Seb and guided by Jimmy, who is well known in the region for being one of the first locals to guide foreign trekkers across the Zanskar Mountains, came from Barandy Nala, where the Manali-Leh road leaves the valley and starts its dramatic climb to the Lachulung Pass. I took a longer route over the Morang La, which had stopped me in the late spring a few months earlier, in order to finish one of my best treks ever: from Central Ladakh to Zanskar.

Tsarab, whose source is among the glaciers of the Great Himalaya, is already a huge river in Tsokmitsik, but Hormoche, where I managed to cross, is well below that. In autumn, when the current decreases significantly so the amount of sediment carried by the river is lower, the water changes colour from muddy grey to the kind of turquoise which most of us imagine exists only on much-adjusted photographs. Believe me, it is real!

However, this lively colour of the river would not mean so much here if the diverse shades of grey, beige, yellow, orange and other hues of the bare desert mountains were not so obvious. Slopes are dry and often completely barren, but riverbeds are not – shrubs and perennials are abundant and willow bushes cover some areas. In autumn they are magnificently colourful, adding much to the beauty of this austere landscape.

⌃ On the high route between Hormoche and the confluence of the Tsarab and Niri Chu rivers

◁ The Tsarab Chu on the way from Satak to Hormoche; it is autumn and the river displays its rich turquoise colouring
(photos: Radek Kucharski)

The route along the Tsarab Chu is demanding. On the hardest day, two major and three secondary passes are crossed, and a great distance at high altitude is covered. Much of the trail is over a remote area where there are no villages. Hardly anyone is met along the way. Jimmy's group was the only one I saw when I was there on my own, and when repeating the route with my own groups I would often meet no one on a long section at the beginning of the trek.

At the end of the wildest part, the monastery of Phuktal is reached; its location is unrivalled. As the route continues, picturesque Zanskar villages are passed, with the autumn harvest in full swing. Farming methods have barely changed in centuries – they ensure sufficient crops for families to survive, and secure productivity of the land for the future. Animals are used during threshing, and wind helps separate grain from chaff. Songs are sung, and the hard work seems to be done in a balanced and calm manner.

'Open space, boundless views of wild mountains, a vast and serene landscape – and tranquillity'

There's wildlife to observe too. I remember one particular encounter with an ibex in a valley above Phuktal. It stood for a long time, looking directly at us, apparently surprised to see us there.

Some might say there are no major highlights on this trek; no views of well-known mountains, no waterfalls or impressive glaciers, no sharp and spectacular peaks or ridges. What you have is an expanse of open space, boundless views of wild mountains, a vast and serene landscape – and tranquillity. What you gain is the calm and inner peace which few things but long contact with nature can give.

And the rucksack? Well, for a lonely trekker like me, carrying all camping equipment, food supplies for a few days, as well as much photographic gear, lifting the bag above my head would not be possible, and I'd not even consider crossing a big river like that. And the only reason I dared try crossing the Tsarab Chu at all was that I had missed the right way!

▲ The view from Concordia along the Godwin-Austen Glacier towards K2

50 K2 – the Savage Mountain

ALAN HINKES

Often known as the 'Third Pole', the Baltoro Glacier region in the Karakoram range of Pakistan is home to K2, the world's second highest mountain. This stark pyramid-shaped peak is the true mountaineer's first prize, the Gold Medal. At 8611m, it is not much lower than Everest but much more difficult. The trek to Base Camp is more remote and arduous; it has worse weather, more avalanches and rockfalls, and more technical climbing.

My first view of K2 was from Concordia, where the Baltoro Glacier and the Godwin-Austen Glacier meet. I was transfixed and captivated, and felt a calling that I had to climb this sheer, breathtakingly perfect-looking mountain. I was acutely aware

'I had to climb this sheer, breathtakingly perfect-looking mountain'

that this was no rosy-eyed illusion, as it looked unforgiving, serious and harsh. Dubbed the Savage Mountain, K2 is a real challenge.

Eventually, after three expeditions and attempts over a three-year period, I summited and got back down in one piece. You could say that I dedicated, or donated, three years of my life to K2.

On each of my three expeditions, several climbers were killed and injured; on my final successful expedition, when I reached the top, only five climbers summited and eight died. For me, no mountain is worth a life; the summit is only a bonus and coming back is a success. Also, no

130

mountain is worth having a finger or toe amputated due to frostbite, and I have taken care of all my digits.

In the end I made a solo push for the summit on the same day as two Dutch and two Pakistani mountaineers, on 17 July 1995.

After a two-week trek to BC and three weeks acclimatising, I set off at 3am on the final 600m from a bivouac on the Shoulder at 8000m. It took me 15 hours of serious and very exposed climbing, with a 3000m drop to BC, to reach the summit. I had pushed the envelope of endurance and safety and now would be descending alone in the dark. I spent too long on the summit, but I wanted to linger and appreciate what must be the most inhospitable spot on the planet. As the sun dropped below the horizon and the temperature plummeted, K2 cast a huge triangular shadow across the earth.

Usually it is best to spend only a few minutes on a summit above 8000m, as you are dying in the oxygen-depleted atmosphere. Five minutes is long enough; I spent nearly an hour.

'My head ached and my body felt like it was being crushed in a vice'

My head ached and my body felt like it was being crushed in a vice. Climbing at extreme altitude is agony. Torture. Yet even through that haze of suffering, my oxygen-starved brain was aware of the intense seriousness of my situation. No celebration was due yet. Some of the world's best climbers have died descending K2, even in daylight and good weather. I was completely alone and in the dark with only a head torch to light my way down, and the temperature was a perilous minus 30°C or lower. As nightfall engulfed me, I tore myself away from the summit and, summoning deep reserves of stamina and energy, began the hazardous descent. Pushing myself to the limit and concentrating intensely, I reached the relative safety of my bivouac on the shoulder at 10pm. Exhausted, I crawled inside my tiny tent to rest and melt snow for water. I was massively dehydrated.

My epic was not finished and still no celebration was due, for I still had 2500m of dangerous descent to the safe haven of BC; but alone in my tent at 8000m in the death zone darkness, I said 'Thank you' out loud to someone, perhaps a greater being.

▼ Alan Hinkes on the summit of K2 with a photo of his daughter Fiona – a reminder to get down safely (photos: Alan Hinkes)

MISHAPS AND MISADVENTURES

We all have them – days when things just don't go to plan, when something goes awry, there's a mishap, a lost opportunity. A day, perhaps, when you find yourself in the wrong place at the wrong time. Or simply in the wrong clothing. Some days are so full of woes you wonder why you bothered to get out of bed in the first place. Some of the misadventures we have when 'out there' can be amusing in retrospect, a tale to tell in the pub, a laugh at our own expense. Or they can be literally life-changing; nothing to laugh about at all, but an experience to survive, to unpick in order to discover how or why it happened, and to learn from.

All our authors spend lengthy periods away from home, having daily experiences, adventures and misadventures while researching the routes they write about. Getting lost so their readers don't is just a minor part of a guidebook writer's job description. But acting as a human lightning conductor and being caught in an avalanche are both way off the page and not to be mimicked as a way to true adventure...

Members of the Lochaber Mountain Rescue
Team in action (photo: Mike Pescod)

Making a splash

KEV REYNOLDS

I never did get the shot of Piz Buin I wanted. If a picture is worth a thousand words, the one I had in mind would have saved at least a couple of pages of text.

Piz Buin stands on the Swiss–Austrian border, the most prominent of the Silvretta Alps. Its Austrian flank is heavily glaciated, but the Swiss side is by far the most attractive: a rocky cone-like peak rising from a deep U-shaped saddle – or so it appears from Val Tuoi and the hut which sits at its feet.

I was there one summer to update my guide to walks in the Engadine Valley. Having begun in the upper valley where I'd worked in my 20s, I made my way north-eastwards, ticking off routes day after day. When I'd finished in the national park, just two side valleys were left to check before summer ran out and it would be time to go home to face a winter at the computer.

That old favourite, Val Tuoi, was saved for last.

Halfway into the valley, I saw the picture I wanted: Piz Buin soaring above the meadows, a white-flecked river tumbling over rocks in its bed below to my left. With Piz Buin as the main focus of attention, the river's snaking course would lead the eye towards it. But through the viewfinder, the composition was not quite right. For preference, the river should be on the right of the picture, not the left. So I should be on the opposite bank.

There was no bridge, but I figured that a few more-or-less strategically placed rocks could be used as stepping stones. The first proved easy, the second was a bit wobbly and balance was only retained with the help of my Leki stick. The river was deeper between the second and third rocks and the distance a little more than I'd have liked, so I extended my stick to its full length, took a deep breath, then sprang forward using the trekking pole for support.

As my weight came on it, the Leki stick contracted, the two extended sections slid back into their sleeves – and I was pitched head first into the river.

I never did get my classic shot of Piz Buin. Instead, I took a slice out of my arm and had an early bath. Fully clothed.

➤ Val Tuoi, with Piz Buin enticing at its head (photo: Kev Reynolds)

Struck by lightning

DAN BAILEY

The first route I went out to research for my guidebook on Scotland's mountain ridges might have been my last. All true adventures involve the unexpected, it's been said. We could certainly never have anticipated what was about to happen.

In a bitter wind carrying hints of sleet, we headed for the Cobbler and the South-East Ridge of South Peak, a mountaineering rock climb-cum-scramble in the Southern Highlands. Making good time, we were soon starting up the Arête, a continuation climb leading on to Centre Peak – all great fun, and with no hint of impending mortality. While Jan led the final tower, an ugly wall of cloud cruised our way. Sleet fell in earnest as we coiled ropes on the sharp summit block. We then slipped onto the standard scrambling route, a narrow ledge and a little rock window leading to easy ground.

The best shelter was on this ledge. Here we perched, pleased to have found the only dry patch. As Jan reached to offer me a cup of soup, there was a sudden almighty bang and a tremendous jolt, throwing us both into the air – although fortunately not off the edge. My ears rang, my heart raced; the soup had vaporised.

I was nonplussed. Was someone bombing us? Was this the world's first case of exploding soup? Jan was quicker off the mark, yelling at me to 'Get *** moving!' As my whole body was buzzing and I couldn't feel my limbs, this was easier yelled than done. We staggered to safety, babbling in disbelief.

We'd just been struck by lightning!

I noted a faint burning smell. It was coming from me. We headed down fast, leaving damage assessment for later. There had been no warning – no preceding rolls of thunder, no hair-raising buzz; just the one big bang. What were the odds? Back at the car I peeled off layers, each pierced like a bullet hole. At the sight of my back, Jan muttered something unprintable. Colourful concentric rings had been seared into me, like a target. There were more burns on my foot and on my leg where the blast had exited – thankfully no higher!

We drove home to Edinburgh for a night of minor celebrity in A&E. It's not often junior doctors get to treat lightning victims, apparently. Strikes can do all sorts of awful damage, but thankfully some external burns were the worst of it for us. The doctors were amazed at our luck. The current must have missed my heart by centimetres – it could have been so much worse.

'Was someone bombing us? Was this the world's first case of exploding soup?'

Travels in Iceland

PADDY DILLON

Adventures happen to other people, not to me. I plod along and enjoy my time outdoors, but there are no nasty accidents, no life-or-death situations. There are times when things don't go to plan, or even go horribly wrong, but they always sort themselves out in the end. Maybe I lead a charmed existence!

I'd finished exploring around Iceland's popular Mývatn, and had become consumed by a desire to visit somewhere really remote – Hornstrandir – in the extreme north-west. You can't get there by road or air, but you can get a ferry from Ísafjörður. My problem was getting from Mývatn to Ísafjörður, because the buses clearly weren't going to connect, and one of those buses only ran three times a week.

As always in these situations, I stand by the side of the road, thumb outstretched, and hope for the best. It didn't take long for hope to fade. There was little traffic, even on the main road, with long waits and short lifts. When I reached the junction where I'd planned to intercept the bus to Ísafjörður, the bus had long gone.

> 'A woman...plied me with colourful buns, which I accepted'

It rained as I cowered for shelter behind a road sign, and this road was very quiet. One man stopped and clearly had no room in his vehicle, which was crammed with boxes, but he offered me food, which I declined. A woman with a car full of children, apparently travelling to or from a party, plied me with colourful buns, which I accepted. A trucker dropped me beside a campsite in a rising gale, but I decided to continue, regretting that decision as it got dark and the gale intensified. My map said I could walk miles to a roadside emergency shelter, but I was picked up beforehand and treated to a night in a draughty building that a Danish couple were renovating.

The thing about hitchhiking through the Westfjords is that the scenery is spectacular, but it takes forever to get round each fjord, and after a while they all start to look the same. Eventually, I reached Ísafjörður and went to the ferry office. The man checked his Hornstrandir paperwork and told me that he only had space for one person, for a sailing in one hour, and if I took that then I wouldn't be able to return for six days.

What could I say, except, 'How much for a ticket, and where can I buy six days of food?'

▼ Hornstrandir, in Iceland's remote north-west (photo: Paddy Dillon)

Close encounter of
the Germanic kind

GUY HUNTER-WATTS

When I was contacted by Clare Balding's agent to let me know that Clare would like to join me on a hike in Spain for her Radio 4 *Ramblings* programme, I was delighted. It would be a great occasion to get some welcome publicity for my walking guides and fun to meet one of the UK's best-known sports commentators.

After meeting for coffee with Clare, her sound engineer and producer, the four of us set off on one of my favourite walks, which threads its way through some of Europe's most stunning karst formations, close to Montejaque.

After about an hour of hiking, up ahead we spied two other walkers who had stopped for a break beneath a centenarian oak. As we approached, I was pleased to see that they were peering at a copy of

> 'They would, I hoped, go on to heap lavish praise upon the guidebook'

one of my guides. Clare shouted a cheery 'Morning!' before asking our fellow ramblers where they were from, and where they were heading. 'We are German,' they replied, 'and we are following a walk in this book.'

They would, I hoped, go on to heap lavish praise upon the guidebook. It would make for a great soundbite on the programme, and my sales on Amazon would soar vertiginously as a result.

Alas, it was not to be. 'But we are not enjoying the walks,' continued our Teutonic hiker, 'this man Watts walks too fast. He chooses nice trails but there is no waymarking. In Germany our trails are much clearer.' Smiling wryly, Clare went on to say, 'Well, that's a coincidence – meet the author!'

After such faint praise I was keen to defend my book and was about to explain that waymarking was almost non-existent in Andalucía: this was precisely the reason I'd written my original walking guide. But I never got that chance. The bearded male peered at me, opened the book, verified from my mugshot that Clare was not spinning a yarn then said curtly, 'Ah yes, I see that this is him. Goodbye!'

Some months later when I listened to the programme about our walk, it came as a relief that our Close Encounter of the Germanic Kind was not included. Even if I'd failed miserably to impress those walkers, Clare loved the hike. And I was delighted when, for the 100th episode of her programme, she came to choose her five favourite walks from the series and ours made the cut. Waymarking or no waymarking.

◁ Cattle graze amid the karst outcrops near Montejaque (photo: Guy Hunter-Watts)

Rainy lessons in the Dolomites

GILLIAN PRICE

Forcella del Lago is where it all started going wrong. The cloud cover lowered all of a sudden, thoroughly enveloping us and cutting off all visibility. Huge raindrops were pelting down as Nick and I fumbled with our rucksacks and donned rain gear before ploughing on into what was turning into a full-blown storm, complete with thunder and lightning – all rather discouraging for two novice trekkers. After the Forcella, the path took a dramatic downturn – just as well we couldn't see the plunge awaiting...

After edging our way down an impossibly steep scree slope and dodging rockfalls, we finally reached the bottom, dog-tired, starving, frozen to the bone and soaked to the skin. My wind jacket was designed for the Mediterranean and this was clearly the first time it had experienced alpine conditions. I was walking with my arms hooked into my shoulder straps and every time I lowered my hands veritable rivers of water flowed out. As for my legs – I was wearing a decidedly innovative skirt fashioned from a large bin liner I'd cut open, stepped into and tucked into my shorts. But it flapped like a frustrated crow and was quickly ripped to shreds.

> 'I was wearing a decidedly innovative skirt fashioned from a large bin liner'

But the storm was still raging so we had to push on – but now that meant upwards 500m. Thank heavens the red/white painted splashes marking the route were clear and plentiful so at least we didn't get lost. We couldn't see a thing ahead in the low cloud and met no one else silly enough to be out in such ghastly conditions.

What felt like a whole day later we staggered into Rifugio Lagazuoi and sank into seats to enjoy a cup of hot tea. I think I omitted to mention that my methodical partner had drawn a diagram of his rucksack with its contents. But when the time came to find something, he couldn't remember which pocket contained the key list! Needless to say, the contents of both our packs were sodden to the last sock (his water bottle leaked too). As if things couldn't get any worse, the refuge had no free beds so we had to wait for the wind to drop and for the cable car to Passo Falzarego to resume.

Down at the pass, we struck gold at Rifugio Col Gallina. Then a cosy old-style hut, it starred a benevolent cook/manager who dried us out, spread our wet gear around the kitchen and fed us plates of steaming polenta.

No pain, no gain

BRIAN JOHNSON

In 1978, I'd just caught up with Bruce Bryant on the final day of the Swedish O-Ringen (the five-day orienteering event) when I jumped off a small crag into some bracken. Unfortunately, there were boulders hidden in the bracken and I badly sprained my left ankle. This was no problem for a fit young man, and a month later I was on top of Monte Rosa, the highest summit in Switzerland. Little did I realise that the ankle injury would turn out to be life-changing.

Although I was a physics teacher, my life revolved around sport and outdoor activities, and school holidays were filled with orienteering and mountaineering. However, the ankle injury eventually caught up with me: my physiotherapist uttered that awful word 'arthritis' and I had to give up orienteering and, a few years later, walking. My surgeon concluded I would never walk again and recommended early retirement from teaching, which I took at the age of 47. I then took up canoeing and spent much time canoe-camping on the lakes and rivers of Sweden.

About three years later, I had dispensed with the doctors and my ankle improved enough to start playing bowls! On the way back from a canoe trip to Spain, I stopped at a high pass and took a short walk up a small peak. The next day I went for a gentle four-hour hike and, having survived this, decided to do a long backpacking trip in the summer. I selected a small section of the 2650-mile Pacific Crest Trail in the High Sierra, because it was real wilderness but on a good trail, and completed a six-week hike, averaging a measly 8 miles per day. This was enough for me to decide to attempt to through-hike the entire Pacific Crest Trail in 2002. Much to my surprise, I completed this in about five months.

Since then, I've done over 1000 days of backpacking, mainly in the Pyrenees and on the Pacific Crest Trail, achieved a single summer completion of the Munros and an ascent of all the Corbetts and Grahams in Scotland, as well as starting to write guidebooks for Cicerone Press. And in 2015 I returned to orienteering, having not run for 25 years, initially walking but getting competitive enough to become British Middle Distance Orienteering Champion (over 65 age-group) in 2017.

So remember: you'll never win a race if you don't get to the start lane! Life is about accepting challenges and overcoming difficulties. That is why one of my many tattoos reads: 'No Pain, No Gain'.

> 'Life is about accepting challenges and overcoming difficulties'

◁ Having not run for 25 years, Brian Johnson became Middle Distance Orienteering Champion in 2017 (photo: Brian Johnson)

> Striding Edge – featured in
> that first Lakeland Fellranger
> (artwork: Mark Richards)

CD-Day

MARK RICHARDS

Now rapidly approaching 50 years as an outdoor writer, I reflect on a lifetime wonderfully well spent. Creating walking guides and mastering the art of pen-and-ink drawing have been two of the most satisfying components of my life. However, anything to do with the outdoors brings the unexpected...

Grotty weather is clearly a huge frustration, especially when quality photography and artwork are essential guidebook ingredients. Countless are the times I've battled the elements to capture photos and produce sketches.

Sometimes frustration comes not from the weather but from myself. Early in my 'career', when I was still a full-time farmer, I set out on a camping expedition, grabbing precious time away from the farm to research a guide to Offa's Dyke Path with my girlfriend (now my wife of 43 years). Waking on the first morning with a wonderful week's walking beckoning and superb weather forecast, I was so overcome with a bad cold that we unpitched and she drove me home – my eyes were streaming so I couldn't see well enough to drive!

Yet perhaps my greatest frustrations are caused when I am so enthralled by a walk that I foolishly disregard the advice of my trusty 2½in map, which as a solo walker I have always found to be my best friend. For the recreational walker, this can be brushed aside as an adventure; but as a guidebook writer, describing reliable routes is a fundamental responsibility. Time is of the essence, especially with a publisher's delivery deadline looming.

This reminds me of one of the most challenging episodes of my career. After having been actively encouraged by Alfred Wainwright to follow in his footsteps, I had long aspired to create a thorough guide to the fells of Lakeland, based upon my drawings and graphics. So imagine my joy when asked to prepare what was to be the first generation of my Lakeland Fellranger guides for publication. Joy gradually gave way to exhaustion as I endeavoured single-handedly not only to research, write and illustrate each volume but also to prepare every page ready for print within what seemed like an impossible timescale.

The first book, in particular, proved to be a very steep learning curve, and I felt that climbing the north face of the Eiger might have been easier! Having put in a stint of 24-hour days working towards the deadline, at last I got the whole book done – page numbers and all – and copied it to a CD ready to be dispatched posthaste to the publisher. But the weather almost ruined everything...

On CD-Day, our access track was frozen solid and I had to sally forth on foot through blizzard conditions to reach the nearest post office...

> 'Climbing the north face of the Eiger might have been easier!'

Editor's Note

In fairness to Cicerone, Mark is describing delivering the first edition for another publisher and I certainly hope we would be more helpful. But it is true that delivery of a guide project is a major, and potentially stressful, undertaking.

143

∧ Mountain biking in the Yorkshire Dales

< (Inset) A saddle destroyed following a close
encounter with a drystone wall
(photos: Ian Boydon)

The saddle

IAN BOYDON

Sitting while making progress along a route and taking in the views is one of the great joys of cycling; in fact, it is an often underestimated and largely essential element of the activity. It is a great shame, then, that from time to time things go wrong in the relatively uncomplicated task of balancing one's posterior on a saddle.

Granted, to the untrained eye, the long, slender, aerodynamic form of the modern saddle may look like a medieval torture implement guaranteed to extract weeping confessions. However, when this is taken away from the rider – say, several hours from their final destination – even the most razor-sharp, ultra-light carbon perch becomes the stuff of dreams.

On three occasions I've found myself mountain biking in the Yorkshire Dales, miles from my car, with a bike lacking a simple cherished function – that of enabling the rider to sit comfortably while in a good pedalling position.

Once, I was riding along relatively uncomplicated terrain – a grassy bridleway near Sulber – when the bolt clamping on the seatpost failed without warning, causing the saddle to fall off. Fortunately, it did not take me with it, or it would have ensured a swift end to the day's adventure.

'The modern saddle may look like a medieval torture implement guaranteed to extract weeping confessions'

Another time, while riding near Austwick in freezing temperatures, the modern dropper post stopped working. (A dropper post is a type of seatpost that can be lowered or raised using a button on the handlebar, which is useful for getting the saddle out of the way on tricky descents.) It would not have been an issue if it had stopped at full extension. Alas, its failure caused it to lower all the way to the frame every time I tried sitting. This meant I had to either stand to ride, or sit with my knees around my ears while pedalling. It was an uncomfortable and chilly ride back to Clapham.

However, the most dramatic failure of all was self-inflicted. While descending a spectacular bridleway from Old Cote Moor to Litton, I managed to lose traction on slippery rocks. Within a fraction of a second, I collided with a drystone wall – which came off the better. As well as having a very sore shin, I managed to destroy my saddle in the process, and my car, parked in Kettlewell, now seemed very far away indeed.

Several hours later, after riding along Littondale and climbing over Old Cote Little Moor, I finally descended to the car park by the River Wharfe with extremely weary legs and a much greater understanding of the essential role of saddles – the unsung heroes of the bicycle.

Horsing about in Ghorepani

SIÂN PRITCHARD-JONES AND BOB GIBBONS

Once upon a time, trekkers had to camp to explore the Himalaya in Nepal. Dubbed the 'Poon Hill Expedition' by Western group leaders, one popular trek climbed to this Annapurna viewpoint near Ghorepani. Such treks required a full Nepalese crew that included sirdar, assistant Sherpa guides, cook, cook-boys and an army of porters. A further brigade of porters was required to carry the food for the army of porters.

It was the winter season of 1989. Most of the trekkers in our charge came from Australia. In those days, trekkers outnumbered even the Hindu gods of Nepal. We were to lead two groups, one going anticlockwise via Ghandruk and the other clockwise via Ulleri. We would rendezvous at Ghorepani.

Before reaching Ghorepani, Siân's route passes a picturesque waterfall set in a beautiful wispy forest where the lichens are as strong as old rope. In January, the water is frozen and so is the trail. Alas, the lichens could not prevent a talkative Aussie client from sliding headlong down the path as fast as an Olympic bobsleigh, sweeping Siân along with her. Luckily it did not end in tears.

Meanwhile, Bob's group was on the Ulleri steps, a staircase to aid the way. One of the porters had a delicate task – to carry dozens of eggs in a wire cage on his back. How many eggs are needed for a group of 15 trekkers on a ten-day trip, for breakfast and the odd – very odd – cake? As luck would have it, a caravan of mules was on the Ulleri steps at the same time...Suffice to say, eggs did not feature again during the trek.

And so to Ghorepani, which means 'horse water'. This being our third wedding anniversary, the crew 'cut costs' and only put up one tent for us. To celebrate, the cook decided to use the last instant cheesecake sent from London – yes, he had made one before, 'No problem, Didi, Sahib.' After dinner, the dessert was presented to us. The cook had mixed the crumb base with the cheesy topping in one globular mass...

And so it came to pass that after a cheesecake-induced night's sleep, we could not get out of our tent. The sherpas had turned the Force Ten flysheet around in the dead of night with the zip end at the back, and the roars of laughter from the crew could be heard all the way back to Pokhara!

> 'And so to Ghorepani, which means "horse water"'

▼ A typical Nepalese campsite on terraces below Ghorepani (photo: Siân Pritchard-Jones)

Avalanche

MIKE PESCOD

In 2004 I made a decision to do some ice climbing under building cornices on Aonach Mòr. The cornice collapsed and triggered an avalanche above me. I had climbed about 30m and was placing anchors for a belay when the avalanche hit and carried me all the way back to the bottom of the route.

I broke my back, my pelvis, my ankle and some ribs. The people I was with were brilliant and called 999 straight away. It took five hours for the rescue team to get to us, by which time the weather was terrible. It was a really difficult job getting me out and I am completely indebted to the rescue team and their skills.

Being in hospital in Glasgow for nearly six weeks, I had plenty of time to analyse what went wrong. To start with, I put it down to being in the wrong place at the wrong time; I was just unlucky. If I did exactly the same again, I thought, I would not get avalanched. It was just a matter of chance – but what were the chances? One in ten or one in a hundred? But if this was the case for every day I went climbing, whether or not I came home was just down to luck. That's no way to live and work. I can't have the future of my career and my family reliant on good luck.

So instead I looked at all the small decisions that led me to be at that place at that time, and there was a long list of human factors that influenced my decision-making. I had a good plan at the start of the day that I should have stuck to, but I changed it because of things like: using the gondola and being committed to climbing on Aonach Mòr; being new to guiding and feeling that I had to deliver something special; familiarity with the climb and the crag. None of these had anything to do with the snow in front of me, which was clearly telling me not to attempt the route.

With more experience, I am now far more able to make decisions based on the conditions, even if that means my clients are disappointed. We must always be very aware of the human factors that lead us to make poor decisions. The climbs will always be there; make sure you are, too.

'The climbs will always
be there; make sure
you are, too'

A cornice above Morwind – danger in waiting (photo: Mike Pescod)

An adventurous bunch – CONTRIBUTING AUTHORS

‹ From the islands of Croatia to the mountains of Montenegro, **Rudolf Abraham** knows an adventure when he sees one. He has written several guidebooks for Cicerone, the latest of which is *The Peaks of the Balkans Trail*.

‹ **Dan Bailey** is the author of *Scotland's Mountain Ridges* and *Great Mountain Days in Scotland*. A Londoner by birth, he is happier as an adopted Fifer, where he lives with his wife and two budding young mountaineers.

‹ **Grant Bourne** is a New Zealander whose fascination with other lands and cultures has taken him through much of Asia, Africa, the Near East and Europe. He co-wrote *Walking in the Bavarian Alps* with his wife, **Sabine**.

‹ **Ian Boydon** has mountain biked in the Lake District and Yorkshire Dales for almost 20 years – starting out as a 15-year-old on a fully rigid Diamondback. He is the author of *Mountain Biking in the Lake District* and *Mountain Biking in the Yorkshire Dales*.

‹ A professional writer, lecturer and photographer specialising in mountain, outdoor and travel topics, topography, prehistoric sites, historical interests and travel worldwide, **Hamish Brown** knows a thing or two about adventure. He is the author of *The High Atlas: Treks and climbs on Morocco's biggest and best mountains*.

‹ An ordained minister from Seattle, Washington, **Sandy Brown** planned his first trek on the Camino de Santiago after reading Paolo Coelho's *The Pilgrimage*. He has since walked thousands of kilometres on pilgrim trails and written Cicerone's *The Way of St Francis*.

‹ For **Justi Carey** and her partner **Roy Clark**, a lifelong passion for the outdoors was nurtured in the British mountains when they were teenagers. In 2002 they moved to Slovenia where they ran a B&B, before falling in love with Ireland's Atlantic coast. Together, they wrote *Trekking in Slovenia* and *The Julian Alps of Slovenia*.

‹ The author of several guidebooks, **Alan Castle** has trekked and cycled in over 30 countries within Europe, Asia, North and South America, Africa and Australasia. His latest Cicerone guidebook is *The Southern Upland Way*, which showcases the landscape he now calls home.

❮ In 2007, outdoors all-rounder **Rachel Crolla** made history when she became the first woman to reach the summit of every country in Europe. She co-wrote the Cicerone guidebook *Europe's High Points* soon afterwards. More recently she has, together with her partner **Carl McKeating**, fully updated Steve Ashton's classic, *Scrambles in Snowdonia*.

❮ Award-winning photographer **Chiz Dakin** came to cycle touring almost by accident, when after a local photography trip by bike she realised that she'd done 50 miles in a single day with a reasonably heavy load. She's been pedalling and writing cycling guidebooks ever since.

❮ A prolific outdoor writer with over 90 guidebooks to his name, **Paddy Dillon** has walked and trekked just about everywhere. He has a soft spot for islands and at the time of writing, was preparing a guidebook to trekking on the world's largest: Greenland.

❮ A walking enthusiast with a passion for conservation, cricket and real ale, **Mike Dunn** has written four Cicerone walking guidebooks to date, the most recent being *Offa's Dyke Path*. His favourite locations for walking are the Welsh borders, the Hebridean Islands and the Lake District.

❮ **Aileen Evans** has spent all her life enjoying climbing, walking and travel. She is author or co-author of several Cicerone guides, mainly to the Lake District, where she and her husband **Brian** have spent many years walking and climbing.

❮ A founder of Cicerone Press, **Brian Evans** is a well-known figure in the outdoor community and has provided walkers with a number of exceptional guides to exploring the countryside, particularly the English Lakes where he is an acknowledged expert on scrambling.

❮ **Bob Gibbons** and **Siân Pritchard-Jones** met in 1983, on a trek from Kashmir to Ladakh. Since then they have been leading and organising treks in the Alps, Nepal, Algeria and Niger, and exploring the world. They regularly return to their first love, Kathmandu and the Himalayas, and have published several books on the region.

❮ **Allan Hartley** has climbed extensively throughout the Alps, in Austria, east Africa, the Falkland Islands and the Greater Ranges in Nepal and Pakistan, as well as the Zagros mountains of Iran and the Hajr mountains of the Arabian peninsula. He has written a trilogy of guides to trekking in the Austrian Alps.

< **Leigh Hatts** is the author of *The Lea Valley Walk*, *The Pilgrims' Way* and *The Thames Path*. As well as walking paths and trails, he has also helped to develop them, with his efforts contributing to the creation of the Bournemouth Coast Path and The Thames Path as a National Trail.

< The first Briton to climb the world's highest mountains, **Alan Hinkes** has had his fair share of adventures. The author of *8000M* is also an accomplished cameraman and documentary-maker, photographer, motivational speaker, environmentalist and mountain guide.

< Author of *Mountain Biking in Slovenia*, **Rob Houghton** has been a cyclist for as long as he can remember. His first bike was a Raleigh Striker back when they had fake suspension forks on the front. He has biked in destinations as diverse as Wales and Thailand, Denmark and Singapore.

< **Tony Howard**, together with **Di Taylor**, has spent decades exploring many parts of the Middle East. He is the author of *Treks and Climbs in Wadi Rum, Jordan* and co-author (together with Di) of *Jordan – Walks, Treks, Caves, Climbs and Canyons*.

< **Guy Hunter-Watts** has lived and worked in Andalucía since the 1980s. He is the author of *Coastal Walks in Andalucía*, *The Andalucían Coast to Coast Walk*, *The Mountains of Ronda and Grazalema* and *Walking in Andalucía*.

< **Will 'KB' Janecek** grew up in the US on a small lake in Minnesota, where he learned his love of the outdoors from his father. After a narrow and daring escape from an office cubicle, he rediscovered his passion for adventure activities. He is the author of *Hiking and Biking Peru's Inca Trails*.

< With an impressive list of physical feats to his name, including three thru-hikes of the Pacific Crest Trail, **Brian Johnson** has had many an adventure. He is the author of several Cicerone guides, including *The GR 10 Trail*, *The GR 11 Trail* and (naturally) *The Pacific Crest Trail*.

< An outdoor enthusiast from way back, **Kingsley Jones** has led expeditions all over the world. He divides his time between the Alps and the Lake District, enabling him to guide running groups in the mountains all year round. He is the author of *Trail and Fell Running in the Lake District* and *Trail Running - Chamonix and the Mont Blanc region*.

❮ **Bart Jordans** has been guiding and exploring treks and trekking peaks in the Himalaya, Karakoram, Hindu Kush, European Alps and on Kilimanjaro since 1984. He is the author of *Trekking in Bhutan*, and a contributor to *Trekking in the Himalaya* and *Everest: A Trekker's Guide*.

❮ Both native Lancastrians, **Dennis Kelsall** and his wife **Jan** have long held a passion for countryside and hill walking. They have written several Cicerone guidebooks, covering areas such as Pembrokeshire and the Yorkshire Dales.

❮ Born in Poland, **Radek Kucharski** has trekked in Nepal, Iran, Pakistan and India, getting to know the landscapes, the people, their cultures and himself. He is the author of *Trekking in Ladakh* and the 2018 updated edition of Cicerone's long standing and successful *Everest* guide.

❮ An award-winning writer and photographer specialising in the outdoors, the countryside, walking and travel, mainly in the UK, **Dr Terry Marsh** has been writing books since the mid-1980s. His most recent Cicerone titles are *Walking in the Forest of Bowland and Pendle* and *Walking on the Isle of Man* (second edition).

❮ A mountain guide with extensive winter ski mountaineering experience, **Bill O'Connor** spends at least three months of each year skiing off-piste and touring in the Alps. He is the author of *Alpine Ski Mountaineering Vol 1 – Western Alps* and *Alpine Ski Mountaineering Vol 2 – Central and Eastern Alps*.

❮ **Mike Pescod** has been on climbing adventures all over Europe as well as in Russia, Tajikistan, Nepal, East Africa and Peru. He has been on Ben Nevis over one thousand times. Literally. He is the author of *Winter Climbs Ben Nevis and Glen Coe*.

❮ Author of more walking and trekking guides than you can shake your walking pole at, **Gillian Price** specialises in adventure, Italian style. This inevitably involves some gastronomical delight. She lives in Venice with her partner, the map-drawing wonder man, **Nicola**.

❮ A freelance writer and lecturer **Kev Reynolds** is also a prolific compiler of Cicerone guidebooks. His first, *Walks & Climbs in the Pyrenees* appeared in 1978. It is now in its sixth edition. When he's not off on an adventure, he can be found at home in the 'Kentish Alps'.

〈 A former farmer, **Mark Richards** wrote his first walking guidebook with the direct encouragement of Alfred Wainright. He is the author of the Lakeland Fellranger series, plus several other guidebooks, including *Great Mountain Days in the Lake District* and *Hadrian's Wall Path*.

〈 A man of many talents, **James Rushforth** is an award-winning photographer as well as a professional climber, mountaineer, skier and high-liner. He is the author of *Ski Touring and Snowshoeing in the Dolomites* and *Via Ferratas of the Italian Dolomites Volume 1*.

〈 A chartered civil engineer with a passion for the outdoors, **Jim Ryan** loves an adventure. He is based in Ireland and is the author of *Aconcagua and the Southern Andes* and *The Mountains of Nerja*.

〈 In 2014, **Phoebe Smith** became the first woman to camp at all the extreme points of mainland Britain on consecutive nights. Needless to say in 2015 she was a finalist in the 2015 National Adventurer Awards. Author of *The Book of the Bothy*, she is also award-winning editor of *Wanderlust* travel magazine.

〈 Author of Cicerone's *Kilimanjaro*, **Alex Stewart** has a particular interest in Africa and a passion for mountains. All his adult life he has walked in them, written about them and photographed them. His first ascent of Kilimanjaro was in 1999; he has been drawn back to the 'Roof of Africa' many times since.

〈 Born into an energetic fell walking family, **Ronald Turnbull** was primed from an early age to embrace adventure. He is the author of numerous Cicerone guides, including *Walking Loch Lomond and the Trossachs* and *The Book of the Bivvy*.

‹ An enthusiastic long-distance walker and cyclist, **Mike Wells** has walked and pedalled in just about every corner of the globe. His most recent Cicerone guides include: *Cycling London to Paris* and *The Rhine Cycle Route*.

‹ After a short commission in the Army, **Jeff Williams** trained in paediatric medicine and worked as a consultant paediatrician in North Wales for 30 years. During that time he wrote several walking and climbing guides, including Cicerone's *Walking in the Drakensberg*.

‹ After many years of climbing and road running, **Joe Williams** has since turned his focus to mountain ultra running. He also enjoys playing the classical guitar, and has an unnatural aversion to swimming. Joe is Cicerone's Business Development Manager.

‹ **Jonathan Williams** is Cicerone's Publisher and MD. He spends far too much time in the office but escapes whenever possible to go exploring, and to collect ideas for future guides. Although he has walked in most European countries and plenty elsewhere, there are still many more places to visit.

‹ **Madeline Williams** lives in London and works for the Civil Service. She suffers from hill and green space deprivation, and tries to escape the city as much as possible.

‹ In 1979, after returning from a spell in the early Dubai building boom, **Loraine Wilson** swapped life as an Architectural Assistant for trek leading, mainly in the mountains of Greece. She is the author of *The High Mountains of Crete: The White Mountains, Psiloritis and Lassithi Mountains*.

The Cicerone Team

Photo credits and captions

Pages 2–3

The view south-west from Ben Nevis on a perfect early spring day in Scotland (Dan Bailey)

Page 4

The Vacas Valley approach to Aconcagua, Argentina (Jim Ryan)

Page 7

Deep powder on the descent of the lower half of the Valscura Couloir, Italian Dolomites (James Rushforth)

Pages 12–13

The tiny Märjelasee, passed just before reaching the Aletschgletscher, Switzerland (Kev Reynolds)

Page 23

Jumping for joy in the Italian Dolomites (James Rushforth)

Pages 28–29

Upper Eskdale and the Scafells in the English Lake District (Ronald Turnbull)

Pages 46–47

Walshore Dean, more or less where my experience of the Pennine Way began, England (Paddy Dillon)

Pages 52–53

Looking back to the Eiger, Monch and Jungfrau from the path to the Sefinenfurgge above Mürren (Jonathan Williams)

Pages 90–91

An hour after crossing the Larkya La, the descent to Bimtang leads down a long rib of moraine in Nepal (Kev Reynolds)

Pages 120–121

Cerro Fortaleza and Cerro Espada (the spear) above Valle Francés (Rudolf Abraham)

Pages 132–133

The infamous summit block of the Cobbler, Scotland (Dan Bailey)

Pages 152–153

The Mont Blanc massif from the Cabane du Mont-Fort (Madeline Williams)

Page 154

The Grand Combin massif seen from above the Lac de Louvie (Jonathan Williams)

Page 160

Headed towards the Matterhorn at the end of the Chamonix–Zermatt trek (Lesley Williams)

Listing of Cicerone guides

SCOTLAND

Backpacker's Britain: Northern Scotland
Ben Nevis and Glen Coe
Cycling in the Hebrides
Great Mountain Days in Scotland
Mountain Biking in Southern and
    Central Scotland
Mountain Biking in West and
    North West Scotland
Not the West Highland Way
Scotland
Scotland's Best Small Mountains
Scotland's Mountain Ridges
Scrambles in Lochaber
The Ayrshire and Arran Coastal Paths
The Border Country
The Cape Wrath Trail
The Great Glen Way
The Great Glen Way Map Booklet
The Hebridean Way
The Hebrides
The Isle of Mull
The Isle of Skye
The Skye Trail
The Southern Upland Way
The Speyside Way
The Speyside Way Map Booklet
The West Highland Way
Walking Highland Perthshire
Walking in Scotland's Far North
Walking in the Angus Glens
Walking in the Cairngorms
Walking in the Ochils, Campsie Fells and
    Lomond Hills
Walking in the Pentland Hills
Walking in the Southern Uplands
Walking in Torridon
Walking Loch Lomond and the Trossachs
Walking on Arran
Walking on Harris and Lewis
Walking on Rum and the Small Isles
Walking on the Orkney and Shetland Isles
Walking on Uist and Barra
Walking the Corbetts
    Vol 1 South of the Great Glen
Walking the Corbetts
    Vol 2 North of the Great Glen

Walking the Galloway Hills
Walking the Munros Vol 1 –
    Southern, Central and Western Highlands
Walking the Munros Vol 2 –
    Northern Highlands and the Cairngorms
West Highland Way Map Booklet
Winter Climbs Ben Nevis and Glen Coe
Winter Climbs in the Cairngorms

NORTHERN ENGLAND TRAILS

Hadrian's Wall Path
Hadrian's Wall Path Map Booklet
Pennine Way Map Booklet
The Coast to Coast Map Booklet
The Coast to Coast Walk
The Dales Way
The Dales Way Map Booklet
The Pennine Way

LAKE DISTRICT

Cycling in the Lake District
Great Mountain Days in the Lake District
Lake District Winter Climbs
Lake District: High Level and Fell Walks
Lake District: Low Level and Lake Walks
Mountain Biking in the Lake District
Scrambles in the Lake District – North
Scrambles in the Lake District – South
Short Walks in Lakeland Books 1–3
The Cumbria Way
Tour of the Lake District
Trail and Fell Running in the Lake District

NORTH WEST ENGLAND
AND THE ISLE OF MAN

Cycling the Pennine Bridleway
Cycling the Way of the Roses
Isle of Man Coastal Path
The Lancashire Cycleway
The Lune Valley and Howgills
The Ribble Way
Walking in Cumbria's Eden Valley
Walking in Lancashire
Walking in the Forest of Bowland and Pendle
Walking on the Isle of Man
Walking on the West Pennine Moors
Walks in Lancashire Witch Country

Walks in Ribble Country
Walks in Silverdale and Arnside

NORTH EAST ENGLAND,
YORKSHIRE DALES AND PENNINES

Cycling in the Yorkshire Dales
Great Mountain Days in the Pennines
Mountain Biking in the Yorkshire Dales
South Pennine Walks
St Oswald's Way and St Cuthbert's Way
The Cleveland Way and the Yorkshire Wolds Way
The Cleveland Way Map Booklet
The North York Moors
The Reivers Way
The Teesdale Way
Walking in County Durham
Walking in Northumberland
Walking in the North Pennines
Walking in the Yorkshire Dales: North and East
Walking in the Yorkshire Dales: South and West
Walks in Dales Country
Walks in the Yorkshire Dales

WALES AND WELSH BORDERS

Cycling Lôn Las Cymru
Glyndwr's Way
Great Mountain Days in Snowdonia
Hillwalking in Shropshire
Hillwalking in Wales – Vols 1 & 2
Mountain Walking in Snowdonia
Offa's Dyke Map Booklet
Offa's Dyke Path
Pembrokeshire Coast Path Map Booklet
Ridges of Snowdonia
Scrambles in Snowdonia
The Ascent of Snowdon
The Ceredigion and Snowdonia Coast Paths
The Pembrokeshire Coast Path
The Severn Way
The Snowdonia Way
The Wales Coast Path
The Wye Valley Walk
Walking in Carmarthenshire
Walking in Pembrokeshire
Walking in the Forest of Dean
Walking in the South Wales Valleys
Walking in the Wye Valley

For full information on all our guides, books and
eBooks, visit our website: **www.cicerone.co.uk**